HOGARTH

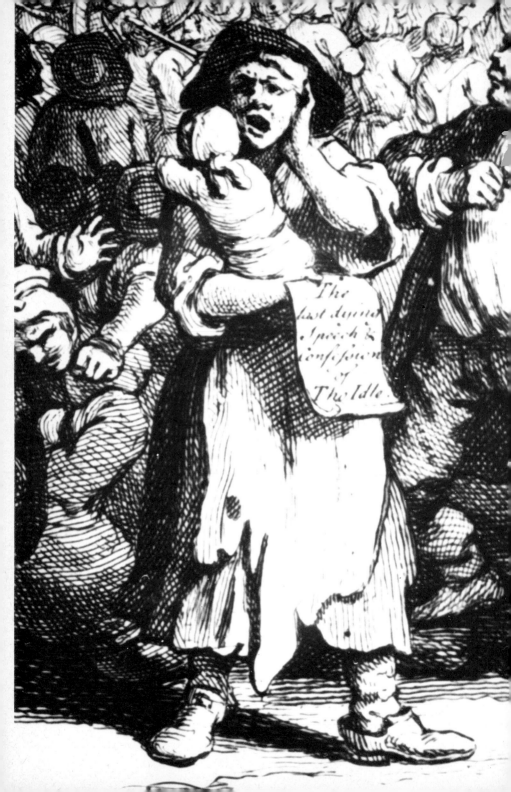

DAVID BINDMAN

HOGARTH

NEW YORK AND TORONTO

OXFORD UNIVERSITY PRESS

1981

To Maureen and Terry Page

1 (*frontispiece*) The ballad-seller at Tyburn, from Plate 11 of *Industry and Idleness*, engraving, 1747 (see ill. 139)

Library of Congress Cataloging in Publication Data

Bindman, David.
  Hogarth.
  (The World of art)
  Bibliography: p.
  Includes index.
    1. Hogarth, William, 1697–1764. 2. Artists – England – Biography.
  I. Title. II. Series: World of art.
  N6797.H6B56   760'.092'4   [B]   80-39785
  ISBN 0-19-520239-2
  ISBN 0-19-520240-6 (pbk.)

Printed and bound in Great Britain by
Jarrold and Sons Ltd, Norwich

Contents

Preface

THIS BOOK owes much of its content to courses on Hogarth and British art which I have given in recent years at Westfield and University Colleges. I can only express a general feeling of gratitude to my students past and present, but I can be more specific in my appreciation of two members of the English Department at Westfield, John Chalker and Peter Dixon, whose misfortune it has been to have offices near mine, and thus be at the mercy of my questions throughout the working day. I have over the years absorbed many ideas about Hogarth from Lawrence Gowing and Michael Kitson, and I must record my gratitude for recent conversations with Martin Butlin, David Freedberg, Andrew Harrison, Patrick Noon and John Sunderland. Without Frances Carey the book would probably not have been started, and without Maureen and Terry Page it certainly would not have been finished. It is to those two, Londoners like Hogarth, that the book is dedicated.

D. B.

London, June 1980

Unless otherwise stated, collections are in London.

Introduction

THERE HAS BARELY BEEN a decade since Hogarth's death over two hundred years ago in which someone has not written a book on him or gathered together a volume of his prints. By no stretch of the imagination can he be considered an unjustly neglected artist. Each generation has found its own Hogarth, and a number of recent studies, notably those by Professor Ronald Paulson, have made available an immense amount of information about his life and labours. Yet our estimate of him has undergone an organic change over the last two centuries.

For his own century and the one which followed he was regarded principally as a great humorist, whose prints provided an anatomy of his own time which could be compared with Shakespeare's picture of Elizabethan England. He was almost universally judged by literary standards, and William Hazlitt's claim that as a comic author he was second only to Shakespeare was rarely challenged. One can cite innumerable examples of his influence upon writers from Fielding to Dickens, and he played an important posthumous role in the rise of literary painting in England in the nineteenth century. By contrast he was very little regarded as a painter, nor was his engraving technique normally regarded as more than serviceable. For most people the Hogarth they knew came from late and reworked impressions of his worn-out plates or bad steel-engraved copies. Even in his own lifetime, with a few notable exceptions, his paintings were very rarely collected, and he himself made the technique of his own prints seem unimportant by claiming that he was too idle to be a good engraver, bringing in French engravers to copy his designs when he could afford to.

In the present century many of his paintings in public collections, such as *The Graham Children* (Tate Gallery) and *The Shrimp Girl* (National *113, 120* Gallery), have been greatly admired, but it was only with Lawrence Gowing's great exhibition of his work at the Tate in 1971–72 that the full spectrum of his achievement could be gauged. He emerged from that exhibition as unquestionably one of the great eighteenth-century painters, a marvellous colourist and an innovator at all levels of artistic expression. In a way this revelation has not yet been fully assimilated, and it is the main aim of this book to reconcile his achievements as a satirist with his prowess as a painter. It was assumed by many writers on the arts after Hogarth's death that great painting was not compatible with a comic sensibility: an artist must aspire to the tragic mode in order to be regarded on the highest level. Hogarth was well aware of such arguments, and fought vigorously against them. Yet while one would no longer criticize him on classical grounds, his enemies did justifiably point to contradictory directions in his art, which reflect in the last resort a highly contradictory personality. He was extremely pugnacious in argument, yet deeply hurt by criticism. He could be notably crude in his judgments, yet he was also capable of remarkably delicate perceptions. We might find his relentless publicity-seeking and quest for notoriety distasteful in this post-Romantic era, but for him the audience were his own contemporaries; their verdict was more important to him than that of posterity.

I have tried to approach Hogarth as much as possible within the context of his own time, and I have made extensive use of his own words, mainly written right at the end of his life in a compilation which was never published nor properly organized (now to be found in a manuscript collection in the British Library), which contains the *Autobiographical Notes* and *The Apology for Painters*. The sentences are not always continuous and the tone is often extremely shrill, but nonetheless the phrasing is usually vigorous and persuasive. I have also drawn considerably on George Vertue's Notebooks, which give an unparalleled insight into the artistic life of Hogarth's London. Vertue (1684–1756) was an engraver who conceived an exhaustive history of English engraving from its beginnings to the present day, and in the course of his work he jotted down his impressions of his contemporaries, of whom Hogarth was one of the most notable. He was admiring of him and at the same time a little wary, so that one gets from his Notebooks a vivid picture of Hogarth both as an emerging artist and as a 'scheemist'.

The Fear of Grub Street

WILLIAM HOGARTH was born in November 1697 in the neighbourhood of Smithfield Market in London, the son of a schoolmaster, Richard Hogarth, who had come from the north-west of England to set himself up as an author of textbooks and dictionaries. There is no record of any artistic talent in the Hogarth family, nor were they related to anyone who had made any kind of mark in the world. Richard Hogarth's contemporaries, if they had noticed him, would have seen his career as a thoroughly commonplace one; a classic example of the phenomenon known as Grub Street. In reality Grub Street was a notorious place of sordid dwellings and cheap attics, which evoked a world of hapless and desperate writers, whose pretensions were not matched by their talents, and who were forever locked in sordid disputes with printers, publishers and each other. Richard Hogarth is not known to have written verse, but he saw himself as a literary man, and he was to suffer the inevitable fate of those who were unsuccessful, by enduring a prolonged period in the Fleet Prison for debtors. The effect on William's childhood can be easily imagined, and he tells that as a boy 'I had before my Eyes the precarious State of authors and men of learning. I saw not only the difficulties my father went through whos dependence was cheifly on his Pen, the cruel treatment he met with from Booksellers particularly in the affairs of a lattin Dictionary the compiling had been the work of some years which being depositid in confidence in the hands of a certain printer . . .' He does not say precisely what happened, but he does claim that his father's fatal illness, which killed him in 1718, when William was twenty, 'was occationd by partly the useage he met with from this set of people and partly by disappointments from great mens Promises'.

As the son of a man who had suffered the harsh consequences of failure, the young Hogarth could not expect to find an easy road to advancement. Although presumably tutored by his own father he would have been cut off by lack of formal education and patronage from the universities and professions, and it appears that despite a precocious talent for drawing he could not even afford an apprenticeship to a painter's studio or an engraver's workshop. In the event he was by his own account 'taken early from school and served [from 1714 onwards] a long apprenticeship to a Silver plate

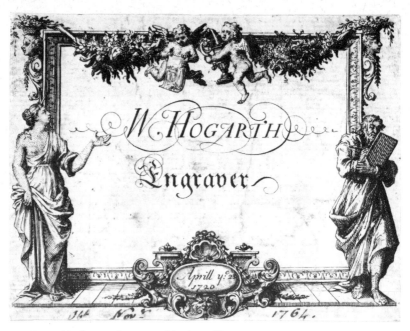

2   Hogarth's shopcard, engraved by himself, 1720

engraver', a branch of engraving which George Vertue described crush-
ingly as 'the lowest degree of that business'. To make matters worse his first
master, Ellis Gamble, was a silversmith of little distinction, and the apprentice soon tired of drawing 'monsters of Heraldry', lamenting 'the Narrow-
ness of this business', and determining to carry on with it 'no longer than
necessity obliged me to it'. As he admitted himself, he was too impatient
to use his time to attain 'that beautifull stroke on copper' which would have
qualified him for the more satisfying kinds of reproductive engraving, and
so he found himself in his early twenties making a precarious and unsatis-
factory living as an engraver of low-priced designs for cheap novels,
2   shopcards, funeral tickets and other forms of ephemera.
       For the most part it was unmitigated hack-work, but it did occasionally
allow some scope for invention. If we look, for example, at the seven illustra-
3–5   tions for Gildon's *New Metamorphosis*, published in March 1724, we can
see that the exercise was not without its benefits. The book itself was a
characteristic Grub Street production, and Charles Gildon was soon after
to be lashed by Pope in *The Dunciad*. It is an updated version of Apuleius,

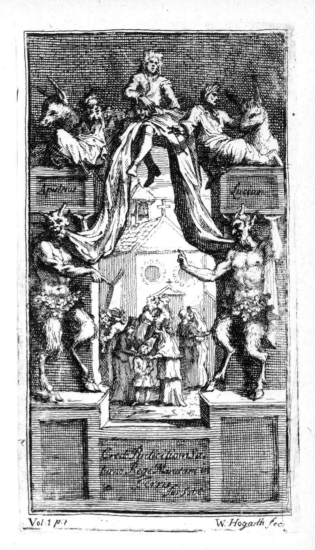

3   Titlepage engraving for
Charles Gildon's *The New Metamorphosis*, 1724

with the ass replaced by 'a fine Bologna Lap-Dog', a popular trivialization
of a classical model. It was originally published in 1708 with illustrations,
and Hogarth has copied and improved three of the original designs, and
designed four new ones himself. They are modest and uneven, but the best
are witty and skilful, foreshadowing some of his later artistic devices. In the
titlepage two satyrs, supporting Apuleius and Lucian, hold a curtain which   *3*
opens up to show an Italian street scene, a motif which looks forward to
the *Beggar's Opera* paintings, and we can see here already the ever-present   *24*

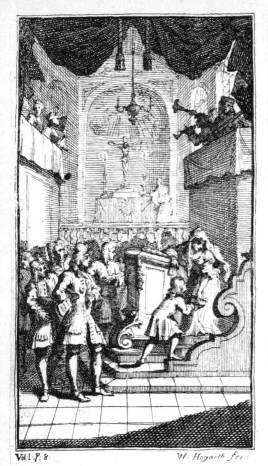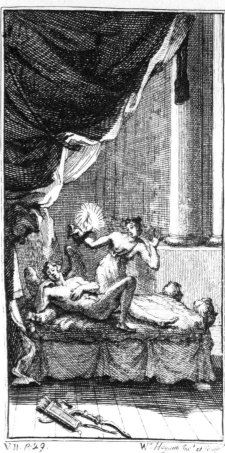

Vd.I.P. 8.   W. Hogarth fec: V.II. P.29.   W^r Hogarth Inv' et sculp

4, 5   Engravings for *The New Metamorphosis*, 1724: *left*, corrupt priests and
gallants celebrate the Feast of St Theresa; *right*, Cupid and Psyche

notion that satire lifts the curtain on the stage of human folly. In the second
4   plate we see into an Italian Baroque church, where a striking effect is
created by the silhouette of the musicians in the gallery against the light
5   from the windows. The most satisfying plate is one that Hogarth appears
to have designed himself entirely, of the traditional subject of Psyche
discovering Cupid by lamplight, which exhibits if not a 'beautifull stroke'
a convincing sense of dramatic gesture and light.

Until he was able to establish himself as an independent artist in his early
thirties Hogarth remained part of this precarious literary world, although

his enrolment in the St Martin's Lane Academy in 1720 would have given him a glimpse of a more elevated role for the visual artist, and a chance to see some successful ones. Nonetheless his role as an engraver forced him in the 1720s into an endless cycle of imitation, inadequate reward and thwarted self-expression. Like his own father he no doubt craved fame and fortune and dreamed of finding a patron who would recognize his talents, but the fact that he was a visual artist rather than a writer made little difference to the treatment he received. His first attempt to proclaim himself as an inventive artist was through political satire; in 1721 he produced for a bookseller two prints, *The South Sea Bubble* and *The Lottery*. The former is a view of the 6, 7 City of London, the inhabitants of which are shown as a motley crowd pursuing greed, vice and folly as they are caught up in the madness of speculation. All virtues and proprieties are broken down, and honesty is punished by the mob in a grotesque updating of the Scourging of Christ. Such motifs can be found in Dutch prints and the work of Jacques Callot, and the hectic incident and grotesque imagery are not alien to much of the political caricature of the time. *The Lottery*, on the other hand, is a model of propriety and spatial clarity, and reveals a knowledge of such canonical works as Raphael's *School of Athens*, which Hogarth would have heard discussed in St Martin's Lane.

The inhabitants of Grub Street had not only to endure the essential misery of the condition: they had also to suffer the indignity of being the butt of the greatest satirists of the period, for whom it was a metaphor of all that was meretricious and false. Pope's *Dunciad* of 1728 contains the most sustained and energetic assault upon 'the Smithfield muses', and Hogarth, after he became established, in 1736 provided an unforgettable image of the condition in the first state of *The Distressed Poet*. We see a poet scratching his 8 head over a poem he is writing entitled simply 'Poverty', which he composes with the help of a rhyming crib. He is shown in a mouldering garret, his wife patiently darning among emblems of poverty and pretension. The implied corollary of poverty, genius, is not there, and the absurdity of the poet's ambitions is underlined by the caricature on the wall of Pope thrashing Curll, and the quotation from *The Dunciad*:

> Studious he sate, with his all his books around,
> Sinking from thought to thought, a vast profund!
> Plung'd for his sense, but found no bottom there;
> Then writ, and flounder'd on, in mere despair.

In Pope's formulation he is a fool who 'sets up for a Wit'; the type of poet who may persuade the 'polite' classes through their own negligence that he is the real article, and thus bring on the reign of 'Dulness'.

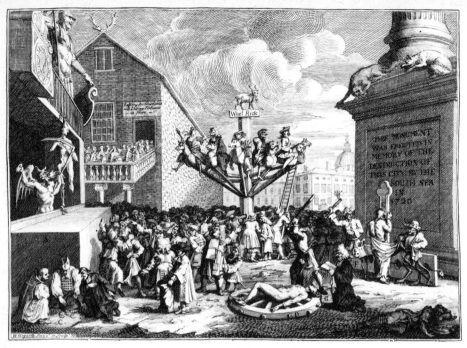

6   *The South Sea Bubble*, engraving, 1721

7   *The Lottery*, engraving, 1721

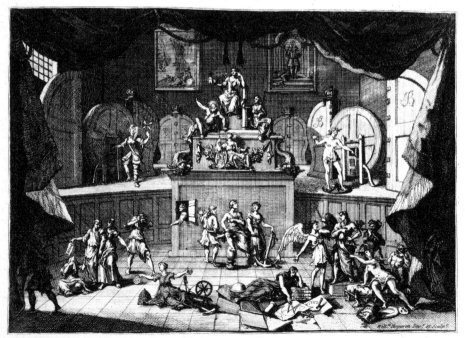

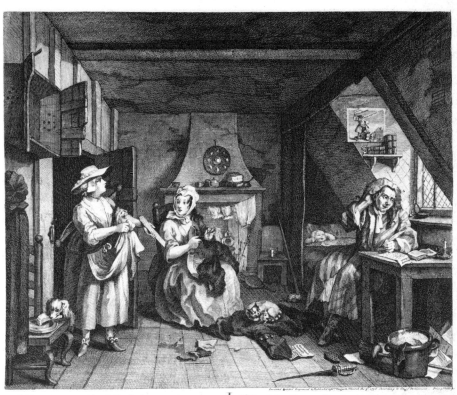

Studious he sate, with all his books around,
Sinking from thought to thought, a vast profound:

Plung'd for his sense, but found no bottom there;
Then writ, and flounder'd on, in mere despair.

DUNCIAD Book I. line III.

8   *The Distressed Poet*, engraving, first state, 1736

Pope's characterization of Grub Street was symptomatic of a feeling in the period that standards in all things were decaying: the cultivated world was being taken over by poor taste and superficiality, which was in turn an index of the decay in morals. Ironically but predictably the Dunces themselves were wont to say the same sort of thing. Aubrey Williams in his book on *The Dunciad* quotes a passage from one of Pope's victims, John Oldmixon, in which the same note of regret for a lost world can be heard:

Good judges foresaw it twenty or thirty years ago, and mark'd the Gradations by which this Decay wou'd appear sensibly. They, probably, made those Reflections from what they had observ'd of the Fate of Poetry and Eloquence; when, after the Age of Augustus, Mimes, Cudgel-Players, and Bears, were preferr'd to true Comedy; the Points of Martial to the happy turns of Catullus; when Sound got the better of Sense, and solid Reason gave way to Tales and Trifles; when the Degeneracy reach'd their Morals as well as their Arts and Sciences, (as it will always do in all Countries) and the Loss of their Taste was follow'd with the Loss of their Liberty.

9   This passage precisely catches the sense of Hogarth's first self-published print, *The Taste of the Town* or *Masquerades and Operas*, which had appeared in 1724, some four years before *The Dunciad*, and could well have been known to Pope. This small engraving is of a street scene in which crowds flock on one side to a Harlequin enactment of *Dr Faustus*, and on the other side to a masquerade beneath the rooms of the aptly named conjurer Fawkes, or Faux as Hogarth chooses to spell it. A sign hangs out containing a grotesque scene from an opera. The common factor in all these entertainments is travesty and deception. A harlequinade cheapens a great old play, a masquerade gives pleasure through disguise, and a taste for them is a characteristic attribute of Hogarth's weak and immoral victims. In contrast to these fashionable pursuits, a barrow filled with the works of the great English dramatists – Congreve, Dryden, Otway, Shakespeare, Addison and Ben Jonson – is trundled off for waste-paper. The verses at the bottom, probably written for Hogarth by a friend, reinforce the stark contrast between the present and earlier ages:

Could new dumb Faustus, to reform the Age,
Conjure up Shakespear's or Ben Johnson's Ghost,
They'd blush for shame, to see the English Stage
Debauch'd by fool'ries, at so great a cost.
What would their Manes say? should they behold
Monsters and Masquerades, where usefull Plays
Adorn'd the fruitfull Theatre of old
And Rival Wits contended for the Bays.

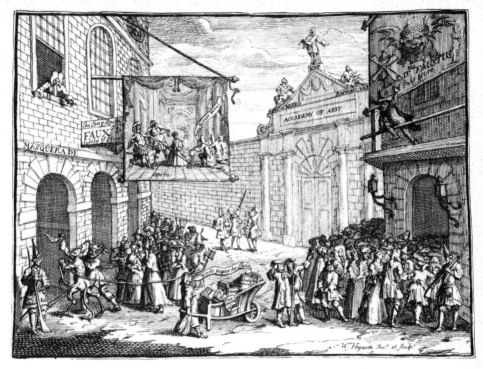

9 *The Taste of the Town*, or *Masquerades and Operas*, engraving, first state, 1724

It is not fortuitous that most of Hogarth's targets were foreigners, like the impresario Heidegger, but it is also significant that he makes fun of the Burlington circle, whose zeal in encouraging the taste for Palladian architecture is here implicitly equated with the decay of old values. In a brilliant visual joke the Earl of Burlington's companion, the architect William Kent (1684–1748), who had begun his career in Italy as a painter, is shown swaggering on top of a classical pediment with Michelangelo and Raphael relegated to the corners as mere supporters. The building they adorn is the 'Accademy of Arts', and three incisively characterized fops look upwards in admiration.

This attack on the Palladians and a tendency to invoke the English rather than the classical past shows that Hogarth was already allying himself with a point of view which would have been shared by the painter Sir James Thornhill (1675/76–1734), who had himself been allied with the 11–13 interest of Sir Christopher Wren, and had been an active member of the St Martin's Lane Academy. Before looking at Thornhill, who was to play a vital part in Hogarth's later career, it is necessary to make a brief survey of the artistic scene in England, which was in the 1720s at a low point of provincialism.

There was no academy as in France to lay down an orthodoxy, there were no places of exhibition, very few places of formal instruction and hardly any books of art theory. It was very difficult to see works of art, for there was no system by which they could be made accessible. There was, however, no shortage of demand for art of most kinds, but understandably patrons preferred to employ well-trained and talented foreigners, who were always available, rather than nurture native artists who, it was believed, would need a lengthy training abroad anyway. Nevertheless in the early eighteenth century English painters were beginning to emerge and assert their claims. At the top end of the profession were the painters of allegorical wall decorations, for they carried with them the prestige of the Grand Manner and they had the ability to create astonishing effects of illusion which, at their most opulent, could create a completely false architectural space and ornamentation out of a plain room. On the whole we are blasé about their achievements, finding them overblown and empty of feeling, and we are unimpressed by their illusionism, which has often by now been diminished by darkening varnish and overpaint. But something of the wonder that was felt at the time even by the sophisticated can be gauged from Defoe's reaction to Verrio's work (now destroyed) in St George's Hall, Windsor:

nothing can be said equal to what the Eye may be witness to . . . 'Tis surprising at the first Entrance, to see at the upper End the picture of King William on Horseback . . . it was so lively, so bright, so exquisitely performed, that I was perfectly deceived, tho' I had some Pretentions to Judgment in pictures too.

With the 1720s and the advent of the Palladians we begin to find an implied criticism of illusionism, and an attempt to confine painting within the bounds of an architectural structure, but one should not underestimate the compelling quality these extraordinary evocations of Parnassus and other mythical realms had for the early eighteenth century.

The predominant style of this decorative painting was French, though the first major immigrant, Antonio Verrio (1639–1707), was Italian by birth. He had been brought over in 1672 by the 1st Duke of Montagu, English Ambassador in France, who had been enthralled by Le Brun's work at Versailles and wished to establish the French Grand Manner in England. Verrio was followed in 1684 by Louis Laguerre (1663–1721), who acted as his assistant at Windsor, and between them they covered enormous acres

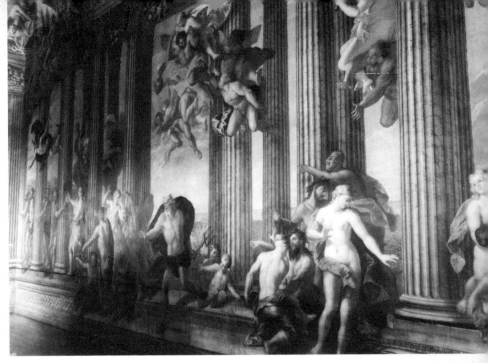

10   Antonio Verrio: wall-painting in the Heaven Room, Burghley House, *c.* 1696

of wall in Windsor, Hampton Court and many country houses. Others like
Louis Cheron (1660–*c.* 1715) also came to England, and many of them
made considerable sums of money. Although most of their assistants were
French, Laguerre and Cheron at least showed some responsibility towards
native artists and both were founder members in 1711 of the Kneller
Academy, the first in England. Furthermore either Verrio or Laguerre, or
perhaps both, were responsible for the training of James Thornhill, who
was eventually to prove a serious rival to the foreign painters and on notable
occasions would beat them to major commissions.

Thornhill is of critical importance to Hogarth, who was to marry his
daughter, from a great many points of view, not least because of his
achievement of wealth and reputation. Not only had Thornhill mastered
the style of Verrio and Laguerre to the point that it is sometimes hard to
distinguish his work from theirs, but he had succeeded, by cunningly
playing the patriotic card, in wresting the two great 'national' commissions
of the period from the fierce competition of, it must be admitted, his
superiors Laguerre and Marco Ricci. These were the dome of St Paul's
Cathedral in London, which he decorated with grisaille scenes from the life   *13*

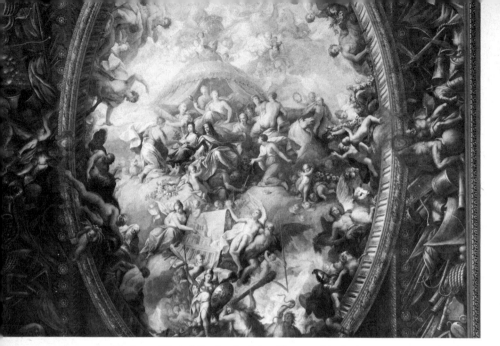

11 Sir James Thornhill: detail of the *Allegory of the Protestant Succession*, on the ceiling of the Great Hall in the Royal Naval Hospital, Greenwich, 1707 onwards

11   of St Paul, and the great Hall of the Royal Naval Hospital at Greenwich, which he covered with an immense series of allegories on the Protestant succession. Hogarth tells us that during his apprenticeship as a silversmith 'the painting of St Pauls and Greenwich Hospital . . . were . . . running in my head', and we need not doubt that they fired him with ambition to reach for such glory.

The St Paul's grisailles and the Greenwich wall-paintings, the latter especially, still have the power to astonish, but one is left with little sense of
12   Thornhill's personality. Thornhill proudly depicts himself within the scene of George I surrounded by his family, and his densely packed sketch-book in the British Museum suggests a dogged and persistent temperament, as if these vast allegories were pieced together from a pattern book, without any sense of overriding conviction. In one design, for example (Victoria and Albert Museum), he has proposed clusters of objects for each corner of a ceiling, and so 'Industry rewarded with Plenty' is shown by objects representing 'Liberty, Trade, Vigilance [and] Merchandise', while a group of military trophies and objects stand for 'Heroick Vertues &c. wth Honour. Loyalty. Love of ones Country. Valour. Prudence. Justice, Temperance.

20

12   (*opposite*) Thornhill: *Self-portrait*, from the royal family group on the wall of the Great Hall at Greenwich, 1707 onwards

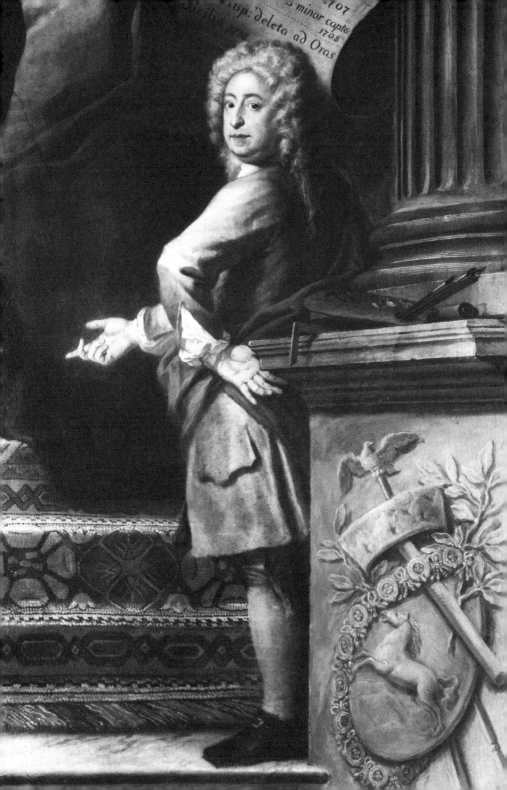

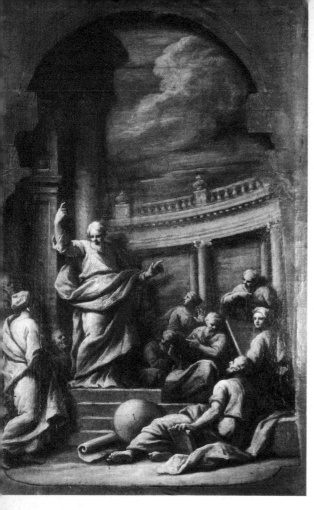

13   Thornhill: *St Paul preaching in Athens*, related to a painting in the dome of St Paul's Cathedral, London, *c.* 1716–20

13   &c.' The paintings in St Paul's dome are duller in effect than Greenwich, being exercises in the manner of the great cartoons for tapestries by Raphael, which Thornhill was privileged to see at Hampton Court, and they lack the illusionistic excitement of the Greenwich paintings.

Thornhill's public face is not the whole story, however, and there are signs of an altogether more human and genial personality in his private works. He was evidently a very clubbable man, and was much addicted to the kind of social and drinking club which was a feature of London life in the eighteenth century. He held gatherings in his own house in Covent Garden, and he made many expeditions outside London from which he brought back descriptive drawings, mainly of architecture. We will return to Thornhill later, but in the meantime it should be mentioned that by 1720 he had reached the height of his reputation, with a knighthood and the post of Serjeant-Painter to the King.

If Thornhill represents the most elevated type of painting in England in the early eighteenth century, there were a number of practitioners, again mainly foreign, of a more down-to-earth kind of subject painting, in which Dutch influence played a greater part than the High Baroque. Here we are faced not with a clearly identifiable succession as one has with Verrio and Thornhill, but with a host of lesser figures, some of whom are barely identifiable today. Dutch low-life pictures, of boors and tavern scenes, were certainly familiar both through earlier examples and the work of a few artists who continued to practise the genre well into the eighteenth century, sometimes in England. Vertue tells us of one immigrant, Egbert van Heemskerk (1634/35–1704), that 'His Gross & Comical Genius succeeded 14 for a long while among us. In most of his Conversations, as he called them, you may see the Picture, & read the Manners of the Man at the same time . . . His Drunken-Drolls, his Wakes, his Quakers-Meetings & some lewd Pices

14   Egbert van Heemskerk: *Tavern Scene*

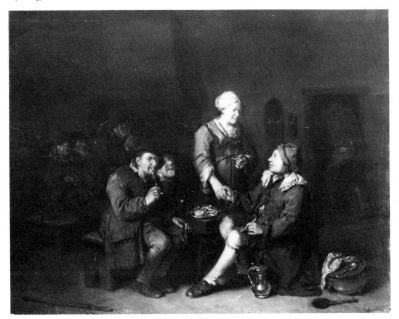

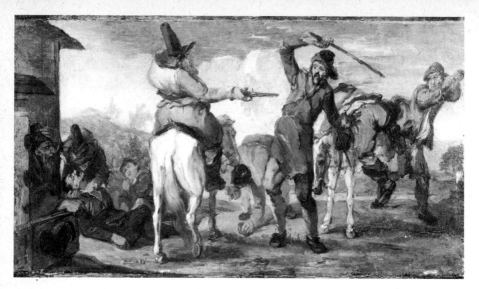

15   Francis Le Piper: *The Combat of Hudibras and Cerdon*, before 1695

have been in vogue among waggish Collectors & the lower Rank of
Virtuosi.' Other painters of genre included Joseph van Aken (1709–49) and
Peter Angellis (1685–1734). Perhaps the most significant and shadowy
development, however, was the emergence in the late seventeenth century
of paintings made as series, on literary or historical subjects. The most
intriguing figure is Francis Le Piper (1640–98), an amateur painter of Flemish
origin, who before 1695 painted a series of panels in illustration of Samuel
15   Butler's *Hudibras*, a poem also to be illustrated by Hogarth. One is brought
even nearer the world of Hogarth with John Vanderbank (1694–1739), who
made many illustrations to *Don Quixote*. The painted series (Tate Gallery
and elsewhere) dates from about 1730, but there is one drawing of *Don
16   Quixote in his Study* dated 1723 (Private Collection), and as a founder
member of the St Martin's Lane Academy in 1720 Vanderbank was a lively
and influential figure. Vertue knew him well and spoke highly of his talent
if not his application, and claimed he would have 'distinguisht himself
above all his contemporys . . . if some loose vain principles had not slipt into
his Morals'. More important to Hogarth perhaps than Vanderbank's
concern with literary subjects was what Vertue called his 'greatness of
pencilling, spirit and composition', and he seems to have absorbed to a high
degree the fluid painterliness of Rubens' oil sketches.

If subject painting, particularly of elevated subjects, or 'History', had a
higher standing among intellectuals it was generally acknowledged that for

24

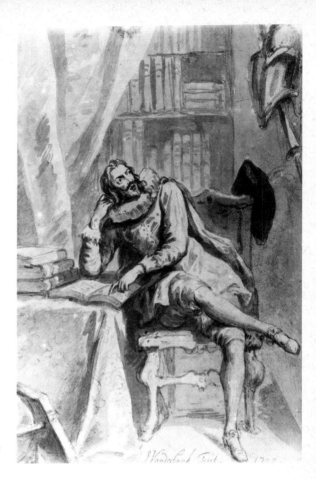

16　John Vanderbank: *Don Quixote in his Study*, 1723

a native-born artist there was a steadier living in portraiture. It might well have seemed to Hogarth upon looking around at the start of the 1720s that there was a greater chance of fortune there than anywhere else. He would have had before him the example of Sir Godfrey Kneller (1646–1723), who had earned enough to build himself a splendid country house, and whose fame and influence would be sufficient to secure for him on his death a splendid tomb in Westminster Abbey. There were, however, major problems for Hogarth. To learn the trade he would have had to undergo some form of apprenticeship, which would have been costly; and he was shrewd enough to see that being a successful portrait-painter was as much as anything a matter of organizing a studio efficiently and playing the courtier, for neither of which he had any inclination.

17

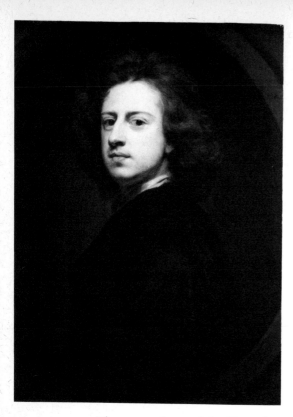

17 Sir Godfrey Kneller: *Self-Portrait*, 1685

18 Hudibras sallying forth: plate 2 for Samuel Butler's *Hudibras*, engraving, 1725–26

9   The connection made by Hogarth in *The Taste of the Town* between low entertainment on the stage and Palladian architecture, represented by the 'Accademy of Arts' in the background, may refer to the fact that Thornhill had recently suffered what was to prove a decisive blow to his career through the activities of the Burlington party, for he had lost the important commission for the decoration of Kensington Palace to William Kent himself. More significant in the long run, perhaps, was the capture of the Board of Works by the Palladians from the supporters of Sir Christopher Wren, among whom Thornhill could be counted. In effect it spelled the end of the ascendency of the late Baroque tradition which had been responsible for St Paul's and so many of the great London churches, replaced by what could readily be characterized by those hostile to it as the import of foreign modes. It seems a crude stratagem to make a snide connection between masquerades, harlequinades, opera and Palladianism, especially given the strong Italian roots of Wren's architecture, but the print reflects the sense of affronted patriotism among those who were threatened by the new classicism.

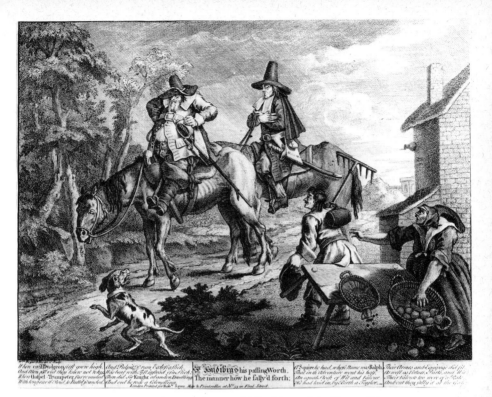

When civil Dudgeon first grew high, | And Pulpit Drum Ecclesiastick | Sr HUDIBRAS his passing Worth, | A Squire he had, whose Name was Ralph, | Their Armes and Equipage did fit,
That Men fell out they knew not why, | Was beat with Fist instead of a Stick; | The manner how he sally'd forth; | That in th' Adventure went his half, | As well as Vertues, Parts, and Wit
When Gospel Trumpeter surrounded | Then did Sir Knight abandon Dwelling, | | An equal Stock of Wit and Valour | Their Valours too were of a Size,
With long ear'd Rout, to Battle sounded, | And out he rode a Colonelling. | | And had as dar'd in Fight, as Taylor, | And both did Fury it alike.
London Printed for Rob.t Sayer, Map & Printseller, at N.o 53 in Fleet Street.

As Hogarth has told us, the popularity of *The Taste of the Town* did not bring him any profit, so he was forced to continue with book illustration. He made a major play for attention by producing in 1725–26 a separate series of large plates in illustration of the famous seventeenth-century verse-satire on Puritanism, Samuel Butler's *Hudibras*. This large and imposing set of twelve plates was printed and sold by subscription through a bookseller, but its relative success probably still did not bring him much hope of escape from Grub Street. He lacked the fineness of touch to reach the heights of the engraving profession, and he had no aptitude in mezzotint which was often used for the reproduction of Old Master paintings and portraits. Fine engraving was in the first half of the eighteenth century increasingly a French monopoly, and Hogarth knew he did not have either the training or the patience to compete. Besides, his own gifts and interests were entirely in the direction of original composition, and the inspiring example of Thornhill and the painters he met at the St Martin's Lane Academy, combined with his failure to break out of the vicious circle of Grub Street by any other means, must have made the mastery of oil painting seem the only possible way of redeeming his inheritance.

18

27

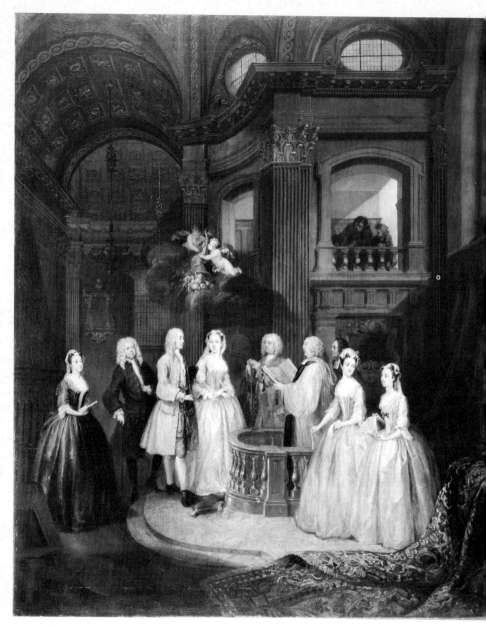

19   *The Wedding of Stephen Beckingham and Mary Cox,* 1729

CHAPTER TWO

Beginnings as a Painter

HOGARTH'S DECISION to become an oil painter was a momentous one, but we know little of the circumstances. We do not know for certain which are his earliest works – there are a number of candidates of varying degrees of plausibility – nor what sort of instruction he received, from whom, or indeed whether he received any at all to speak of. He claimed to have been self-taught, but then artists have always liked to see themselves as free of all influences. Many of his contemporaries certainly believed that it was the case. In a poem by his friend Joseph Mitchell of 1730, no doubt a 'puff' for Hogarth, he is addressed as follows:

> Selt-taught, in your great Art excell,
> And from your Rivals bear the Bell.

On the other hand, Vertue says that Hogarth received at least some instruction, but he also expresses the wonder of contemporaries at the rapidity of his progress:

he by a fluent genius designd & Invented freely several things which he etchd particularly some Caracatures of several persons or affairs of the times. & lastly drew & gravd the sett of Prints from Butlers Hudibrass. afterwards got some little insight & instructions in Oyl Colours. without Coppying other Paintings or Masters immediatly by the force of Judgment a quick & ready Conception & an exact immitation of Natural likeness became surprizingly forward to be the Master he now is.

What this 'little insight & instructions' consisted of we will probably never know, nor are we likely ever to be certain who gave it, but the most likely candidate is surely Thornhill himself, whom Hogarth would have known from 1720 onwards and whose home he must have visited frequently enough to strike up such a close acquaintanceship with his daughter.

If Vertue is right and Hogarth began to take up oil painting after *Hudibras*, which was published early in 1726, then Hogarth's feat in making himself one of the most adept painters in England within a space of a few years was indeed extraordinary; and there is not the slightest reason to doubt this was the case. We can only share Vertue's astonishment at Hogarth's rise from a humble silver engraver to an artist whose 'paintings gain every day so many admirers that happy are they that can get a picture

18

of his painting'. Vertue is undoubtedly right in thinking that Hogarth did relatively little copying of earlier masters, and his belief that he was aided by unusual natural gifts is borne out by what we know of Hogarth's early inclinations.

Hogarth in the early 1720s apparently had worked out his own method of approach to nature, entirely at odds with the consensus at the St Martin's Lane Academy. He claimed that he had begun in the conventional way by copying Old Masters and drawing from life, until 'it occur'd to me that there were many disadvantages attended going on so well continually copying Prints and Pictures, altho they should be those of the best masters nay in even drawing after the life itself at academys . . . it is possible to know no more of the original when the drawing is finish'd than before it was begun.' This led Hogarth to the striking conclusion that to capture nature it is better *not* to draw from it: 'an arch Brother of the pencil gave it this turn: That the only way to learn to draw well was never to draw at all.'

Hogarth proposed instead a kind of memory training and method of shorthand which would allow him to remember what he saw by learning 'the habit of retaining in my minds Eye whatever I design'd to Imitate, without directly drawing it at the time'. This meant looking at the visual world as a kind of language to be learned by persistent experience, much as we learn verbal language. According to his own account he decided he 'should not continue copying objects but rather read the language of them (and if possible find a grammar to it) and collect and retain a remembrance of what I saw by repeated observations only trying every now and then upon my canvas how far I was advanc'd by that means'. We do not know precisely what Hogarth's system involved but he does give us some clues. He tells us that it entailed 'retaining in my mind *lineally* such objects as fitted my purpose best', so it was clearly some process of linear abstraction – a way of reducing the forms of people and things to an easily memorable system of lines, of the kind that is perhaps reflected in an anecdote told by his early biographer, John Nichols.

20

121–123

We will return to some of these questions when we come to discuss *The Analysis of Beauty*, but it is worth repeating that Hogarth began to think about these ideas when he was contemplating a career as a painter, and that this highly original approach was conceived not in isolation but in a context of close discussion and argument with fellow artists. It accounts for the almost complete lack of the kind of sketches we would tend to expect from such an observant artist; the relatively few drawings by Hogarth that survive are crude and inelegant if extremely forceful. The avoidance of conventional drawing put a premium upon spontaneity, for though Hogarth's method may have involved lines it was not essentially linear in

Hogarth boaſted that he could draw a Serjeant with his pike, going into an alehouſe, and his Dog following him, with only three ſtrokes;—which he executed thus:

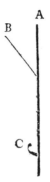

A. The perſpective line of the door.
B. The end of the Serjeant's pike, who is gone in.
C. The end of the Dog's tail, who is following him.
There are ſimilar whims of the *Caracci.*

the usual meaning of the term. The idea of abstracting forms into lines is quite different from using line to make a contour around a form, and it encouraged the painter to think not in terms of precise outline but in a bold painterly fashion. The chief quality of Hogarth's early paintings is not a niggling hesitancy but a bold and free handling, which becomes more accurate as his mastery increases. This can be seen, for example, in *The Carpenter's Yard* (Sidney F. Sabin Collection) which, despite the doubts of some scholars, I believe to be by Hogarth, possibly as early as 1727. The brushwork is broad and open and gives an uncertain definition to the figures, which still contain a surprising degree of individuality and expression. The stance of the two bystanders is humorously captured, and one can see the working of Hogarth's memory system in the way the sawyer turns towards them as if indignant at their condescension. The painting gives the impression of having been pieced together solely from separate acts of observation, with the buildings crudely added around them. Certainly there is no sense of the Raphaelesque composition favoured at St Martin's Lane.

21

The Carpenter's Yard is essentially an experiment in translating observed reality to the canvas, but in the paintings depicting a stage performance of *The Beggar's Opera* by John Gay we can see Hogarth attempting to use his experience as a satirical engraver as well. As such they represent his coming of age as a painter, and the known versions give an indication of a painful struggle for mastery, and a remarkable growth in complexity as Hogarth's command palpably increased; it is astonishing that the fifth version, in the Yale Center for British Art at New Haven, should be dated 1729, when the first performance of *The Beggar's Opera* had only taken place on 29 January 1728. Hogarth may have attempted even earlier to draw together the conventions of stage and pictorial representation in oil paint: *Falstaff* *examining his Recruits* (Private Collection) seems to have derived from a Drury Lane performance of *Henry IV, Part II*, and to have been conceived around 1728. In such pictures gesture and expression are to convey the same richness of expression as words; as Hogarth put it hesitantly in a note to his autobiography, 'The figure is the actor; The attitudes and his action, together with which the face works an expression, are the words that must speak to the Eye and [make] the scene inteligible.'

The *Falstaff* painting still remains a representation of a fictional scene, and the most singular feature of the *Beggar's Opera* paintings, from the earliest versions, is that they include an audience. The success of the play of *The Beggar's Opera* was remarkably fortuitous for Hogarth, for in both sentiment and form it provided a model for a kind of art suited to his gifts. The play was a work of satire, humour and pathos, which, despite its origins in the learned Scriblerian circle, had an appeal which, Pope tells us, cut across all classes in society. The essential idea, conceived by the Scriblerians, was that Gay should write a 'Newgate Pastoral', an opera with music and songs, in which the artificiality of the genre should be contrasted with the essential 'lowness' of the action. All expectations are reversed for satirical effect: the highwayman Macheath is a noble and romantic hero and the thieves a loyal band of brothers, while the lawyers and gaolers are shown as deep-dyed rogues. The satirical point is made at the end by the Beggar author:

Through the whole Piece you may observe such a similitude of Manners in high and low Life, that it is difficult to determine whether (in the fashionable Vices) the fine Gentlemen imitate the Gentlemen of the Road, or the Gentlemen of the Road the fine Gentlemen. – Had the play remained, as I at first intended, it would have carried a most excellent Moral. 'Twould have shown that the lower Sort of People have their Vices in a degree as well as the Rich: And that they are punish'd for them.

21 *The Carpenter's Yard*, ?1727

22 *Falstaff examining his Recruits, c.* 1728 >

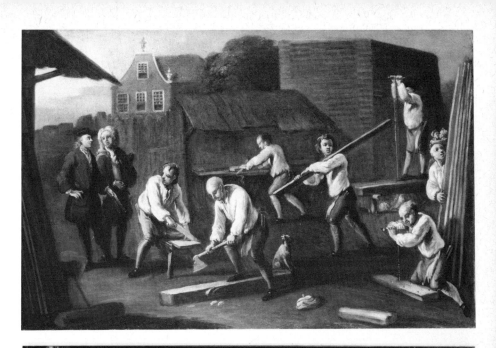

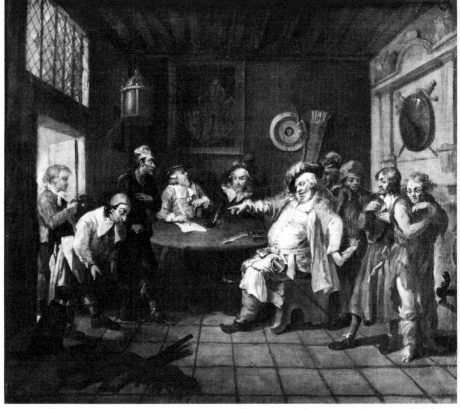

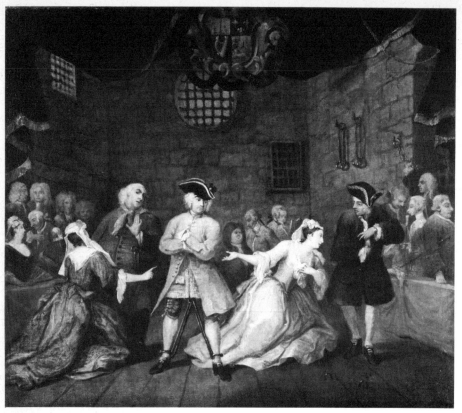

23   *The Beggar's Opera*, version II, 1728

Hogarth grasped from the start that the audience themselves were being satirized and were implicitly part of the drama. In the earlier versions of the painting the actors dominate the scene and are represented as real people, or, to use Hogarth's later terminology, as 'characters', while the audience are shown as caricatures, for the most part pointedly ignoring the action.

    From this *aperçu* all other ironies follow and the development of the composition shows Hogarth consolidating and building upon it. The scene Hogarth has chosen occurs towards the end, when Lucy Lockit, daughter of the gaoler on the left, and Polly Peachum, daughter of the crooked lawyer, beseech their fathers to release Macheath, who stands impassively, not knowing which of his wives to choose. The dignity and pathos of the 'low' character, the highwayman Macheath, is contrasted at this point with the implacable heartlessness of the gaoler and lawyer, who

23

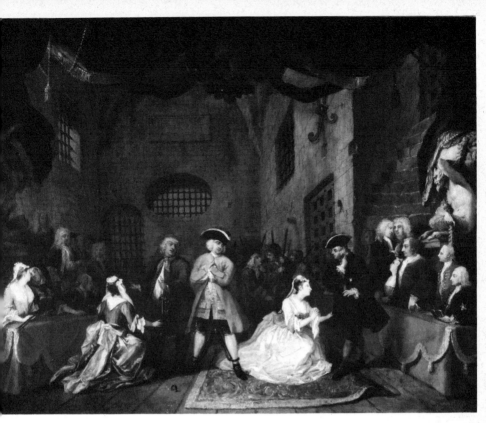

24 *The Beggar's Opera*, version V (Yale), 1729

want to see Macheath despatched as soon as possible. At the same time there is another irony which also comes to the fore: If Macheath is released then we have the dramatically impossible situation of the hero having to make a choice between two equally worthy women. Thus the scene also introduces the final irony of the play which is, as the Beggar puts it, 'To make the piece perfect, I was for doing strict poetical Justice. – Macheath is to be hanged.' Whereupon the player replies: 'Why then, Friend, this is a down-right deep Tragedy. The catastrophe is manifestly wrong, for an Opera must end happily. . . . All this we must do, to comply with the Taste of the Town.'

John Rich, the producer of the Theatre Royal in Lincoln's Inn Fields, bought the first version from Hogarth, and others commissioned replicas. Rich also asked him to do a larger and more elaborate version probably to hang in the theatre, and this is the picture now in New Haven, of which the 24

Tate has a replica painted in 1731. The Yale and Tate versions are more polished productions, and apart from correcting some of the infelicities of the earliest compositions, such as the exceedingly clumsy figure of Peachum, Hogarth has altered the whole scale and brought in an audience composed of recognizable and for the most part lightly caricatured notables. Whether it was Rich's or Hogarth's idea to do this is unknown, but a further range of possibilities is opened up by the relative equality in position of actors and audience: the latter are no longer subordinate but are themselves actors in a drama. The irony of 'real' actors and caricatured audience is replaced by the irony of the audience responding to the actors as real people. With characteristic opportunism Hogarth has shown at the far right the Duke of Bolton looking fixedly at Lavinia Fenton playing Polly Peachum, a reference to the fact that she became the Duke's mistress at the end of the first season. In the earliest versions of the painting a curtain with the royal arms and the motto 'Utile dulce' hangs over the proceedings, giving a clear sense, with the wooden floor, of being in a theatre. The motto itself comes from a passage in Horace's *Ars Poetica* which might almost be taken to sum up Hogarth's double aim: 'But he that joins instruction with delight,/Profit with pleasure, carries all the votes.' In the Yale and Tate versions this is given more point by the words 'Veluti in speculum' (as if in a mirror), and the ends of the curtain rest on statues of satyrs, one of whom points downwards to the Duke of Bolton. In effect this is a return to the motif of the
3 frontispiece to the *New Metamorphosis* of 1724, and it reflects the idea of satire lifting the curtain on the follies and vices of the world, in this case represented by both actors and audience.

The success of the *Beggar's Opera* paintings was enough to convince Hogarth that there was a future in painted scenes from contemporary life and satire directed against the stock targets of the time. In what appears to be a pair of paintings, *The Denunciation* (National Gallery of Ireland,
25 Dublin) and *The Christening* (Private Collection), probably of 1729, he exposes secular and ecclesiastical vice within a setting of human folly. The caricaturist's view of the world as one of fools and knaves has now entered painting, but characterized by an elegance of touch which makes one see the figures, as Hogarth puts it, 'as Actors dresed for the sublime genteel comedy'. The parody is not only of human manners but also of the illusion of painting, for *The Christening* shows a scene which might well have been the subject of a portrait group, but in which everything is out of joint. It is a
19 kind of reversal in mode of his almost contemporary painting, *The Wedding of Stephen Beckingham and Mary Cox* (Metropolitan Museum of Art, New York), where a religious ceremony of impeccable propriety is being carried out. The wit in *The Christening* lies in the inattention of the participants to

36

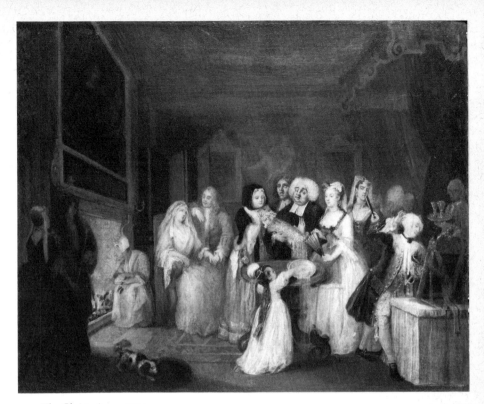

25   *The Christening, c.* 1729

the sacrament being performed: the parson is diverted by the girl standing
next to him, so the little girl has been able to spill the holy water, an event
unobserved by the dim-looking curate and the relative who is only concerned with getting the baby's mob-cap straight. The father is busy satisfying vanity and preening in front of a mirror while in the background,
prefiguring the attentions of the lawyer Silvertongue in the first plate of   79
Marriage-a-la-Mode, another man pays court to his wife. A prudish spinster
and a sleeping nurse by the fire also ignore the spiritual import of the
proceedings, and it is for this reason, even though Hogarth often caricatures
the clergy, that orthodox preachers like the ineffable Dr Trusler could after
his death 'hold the painter forth in a moral light'.

   With the success of *The Beggar's Opera* Hogarth must also have felt for
the first time clear of the threat of Grub Street, and his position was con-
firmed and enhanced by his elopement with the daughter of Sir James

Thornhill, who seems to have been quickly reconciled with his son-in-law. This would greatly have increased Hogarth's chance of getting commissions, but he may not have appreciated how precarious Thornhill's position was becoming. Perhaps in response to having a dependent, Hogarth began to pursue his new career as a painter in earnest, making a systematic entry into the field of the small group portrait, where there were already established and competent practitioners. In 1729 Vertue was able to note that Hogarth had taken up 'the pincill and applyd his studyes to painting in small conversations. or fancyes. wherein he now has much reputation'.

26   We know also from Vertue's description of the painting of *The Wollaston Family* (Trustees of the late H. C. Wollaston, Esq.; on loan to Leicester Art Gallery) some of the reasons for Hogarth's success:

by Mr Hogarth a large Conversation painted of Men & Women of the familyes of Woolastons & containing at least 18 or 20 persons. setting at Cards & Tea & some standing. about 3 foot hi 4 foot 1/2 long this is really a most excellent work containing the true likeness of the persons, shape aire & dress – well disposd. genteel, agreeable. – & freely painted & the composition great variety & Nature.

One can only concur, and although one would not think of *The Wollaston Family* as the liveliest of Hogarth's conversation pictures, it does have a vivacity which his chief rivals, named by Vertue as Charles Philips (1708–47) and Gawen Hamilton (*c.* 1697–1737), could rarely achieve. Hogarth's main aim seems to have been to avoid the woodenness of his rivals' work, and here he was aided not only by his superior powers of observation but by a brilliant and luminous handling of paint. It is the free touch of impasto applied confidently to the projecting surfaces and to the white drapes which creates the sense of flickering movement; but one should not underestimate the artful way in which Hogarth has disposed a rather large party, by separating them into two groups linked only by the figure of Mr Wollaston himself. In effect, by dividing up the numbers Hogarth has avoided the sense of a long line of heads which so often mars his contemporaries' work, and he has unified the groups within themselves by placing them around a card game at one table and the pouring of tea at the other. The two groups are arranged as genre scenes in which the family is disposed with naturalness and a hint of drama, as the players discuss their cards. The moment we are observing is captured within a sequence of events, and the order the painter has established is about to be broken: Mr Wollaston is apparently explaining the progress of the cards to the ladies, but he is about to change his place; a chair is being brought to the card table for one of the standing gentlemen to sit down and thus destroy the pyramidal grouping. There are also hints of

38

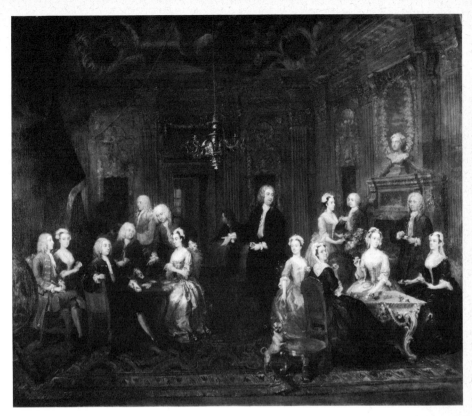

26 *The Wollaston Family*, 1730

amorous entanglements, in the couple by the fireplace and the two ladies playing cards, with the effect that the painting begins to be a subject picture in its own right.

Hints of another genre can also be observed in what is perhaps the greatest of all the conversation pieces, a scene of children acting in a performance of Dryden's *The Indian Emperor or The Conquest of Mexico*   27 (Private Collection) before the younger members of the royal family in the house of John Conduitt, the Master of the Mint. By an ingenious and almost Mannerist contraction of the perspective Hogarth has solved the problem of giving due weight equally to the audience and the players, all of whom are wonderfully characterized according to their ages. The painting is unusually large, and Hogarth has created a remarkably spacious and airy feeling around the figures by a more advanced use of perspective than in the versions of *The Beggar's Opera*, the composition of which it reflects.   23, 24

39

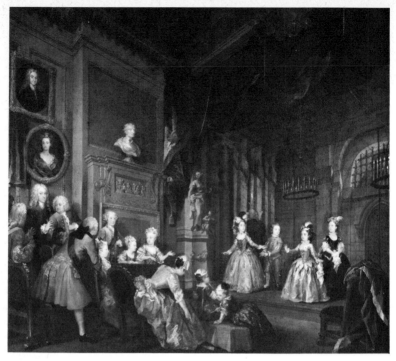

27   *A Performance of 'The Indian Emperor or the Conquest of Mexico'*, 1732–33

28   *The Woodes Rogers Family*, 1729

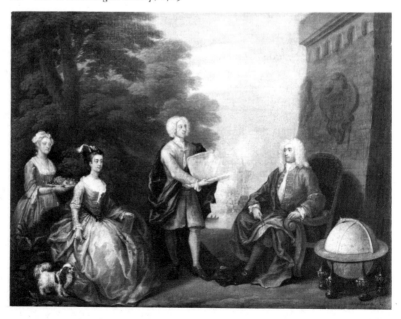

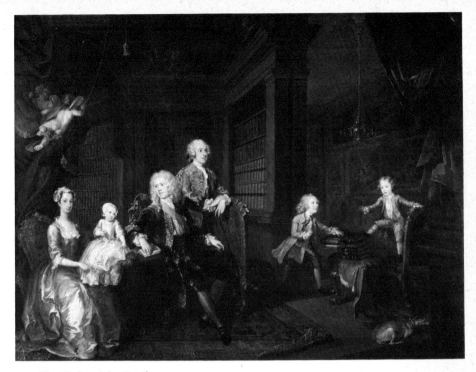

29　*The Cholmondeley Family*, 1732

Hogarth produced a considerable number of these conversation pieces, and he tells us that he preferred them to 'the common portrait' because they gave 'more scope to fancy'. Some of them are actually quite dull in effect, but very few are without some spark of humour or witty comment on the human condition. *The Woodes Rogers Family* of 1729 (National Maritime 28 Museum, Greenwich) has always been regarded as one of the weakest, and certainly the *mise-en-scène* is unconvincing, but it contains an unforgettable contrast between the stuffy and overdressed figure of the lady of the family and the direct, almost insolent, figure of the maidservant behind her. The satirist frequently seems to be on the point of breaking through the surface in these conversations, and children and animals are frequently shown as potentially subversive of the formality of the grouping, as they are in the comic pictures. In *The Cholmondeley Family* of 1732 (Cholmondeley 29 Collection) two extremely vivacious children are playing a game which is causing a large pile of books to topple, one of the boys with it. This is perhaps a comment on the placidity of the group of adults, but it also contains the seeds of allegory, suggesting the ephemeral state of childhood.

41

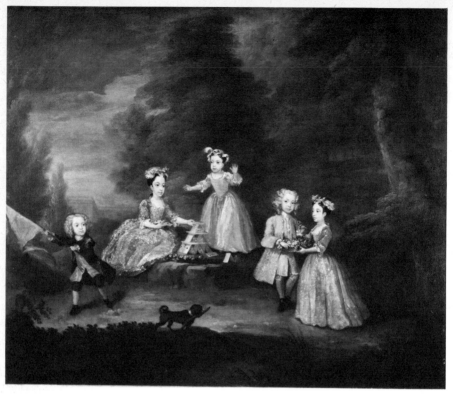

30, 31   *The House of Cards*, I and II, 1730

That idea comes to the fore in the remarkable pair of paintings usually
30, 31   called *The House of Cards* (Private Collection), where groups of children
ape their elders. In each case the pivotal image is one of collapse; in one,
of the house of cards – an obvious symbol – and in the other, of the doll's
table, which a dog is upsetting. The children are clearly real, but the paintings are in a sense parodies of the genre of the conversation piece, and the
aping of adult manners hints at the vanity of human ambition, which is
built like the house of cards on such flimsy structures. It is easy to play the
game of finding precedents in these paintings for later motifs in Hogarth's
31, 43   work, such as the doll's table and the similar motif in plate 2 of *A Harlot's
Progress*, but more significant is the achievement of a visual language in
which action can be conveyed through inanimate objects as well as through
gesture and expression. The imagery of these paintings may be compared
with another pair, very different in spirit but probably painted about the

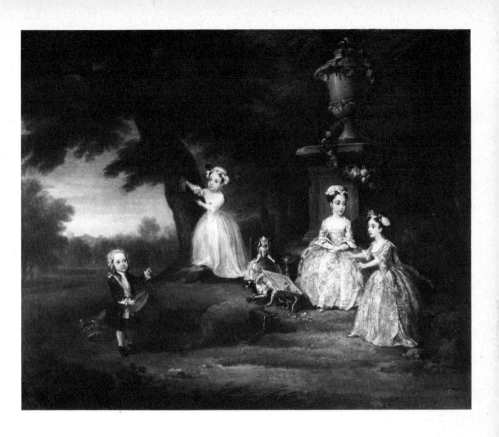

same time, entitled *Before* and *After* (Getty Museum, Malibu). Here the   *32, 33*
action moves from one picture to the other, and the ordinary objects are
again given a symbolic character. The girl being raped reaches out to
grasp a table for support but it gives way. In the scene which follows, with
the roles reversed, the table is now on its side and the mirror lies smashed,
like her maidenhead, and with it the orderliness which had, up to her
surrender, governed her life.

Hogarth's ironical vision constantly comes up against the conventions of
the conversation group, and one becomes aware of subversive elements
ready to sabotage the illusion in each painting. But clearly there was much
for Hogarth to learn from the experience of being a hired painter, particularly through observation of the manners of the wealthy. It must also have
led him to a closer acquaintanceship with the work of contemporary
painters and their European connections.

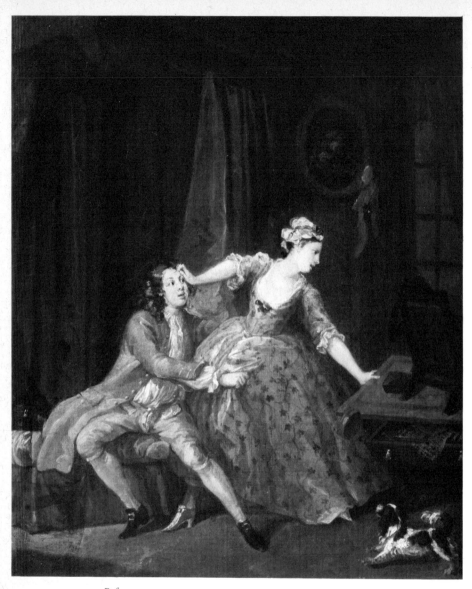

32   *Before*, 1730–31

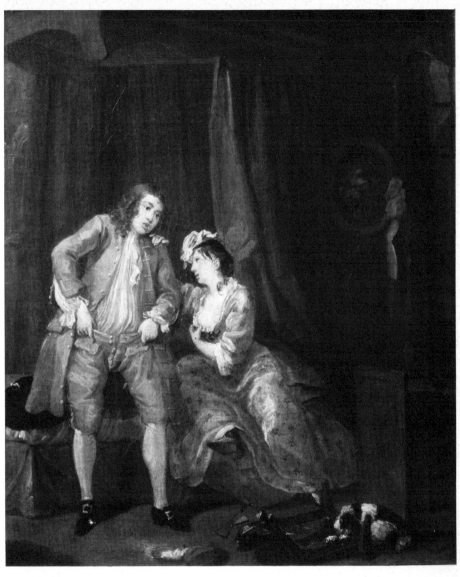

33 *After*, 1730–31

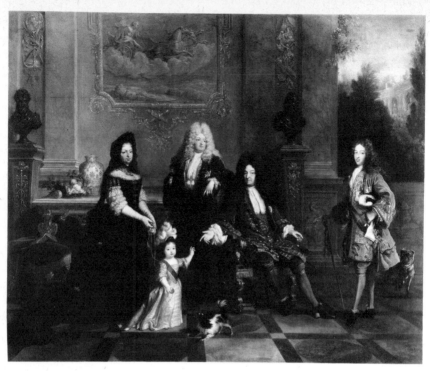

34 Attributed to François de Troy: *Louis XIV and his Heirs, c.* 1709

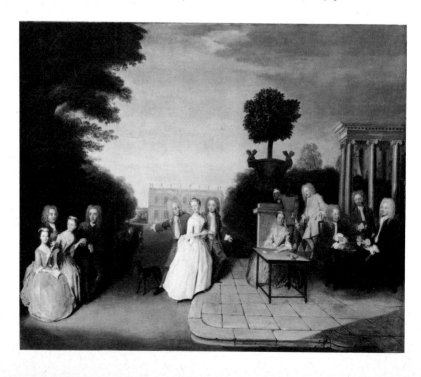

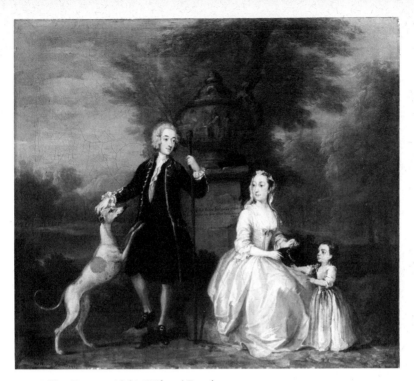

36 *Ashley Cowper with his Wife and Daughter*, 1731

Hogarth cannot have been unaware of the mainly French origins of the type of conversation painting he practised, and Vertue points out prototypes in Dutch and French art, noting in particular a self-portrait group by Nicolas de Largillière (1656–1746) then at Kensington Palace, done in England in 1687. A fine example of this genre is the painting probably by de Troy of *Louis XIV and his Heirs* (Wallace Collection), which is notable for   *34*
elegance of handling and a certain attempt at informal grouping. The still more informal style of the *fête galante* was also known through the work of Philippe Mercier (1689–1760), a follower of Watteau, who had settled in England at least as early as 1719. His painting of *A Hanoverian Party on a*   *35*
Terrace of 1725 (Tate Gallery) is a clear forerunner of the conversation pieces of Hogarth and his rivals, and it may be seen as at a mid-point between the artificiality of Watteau and the more frank and direct spirit of Hogarth. The French influence is most clearly seen in Hogarth's small painting of *Ashley Cowper with his Wife and Daughter* (Tate Gallery),   *36*
in the parkland setting, the conscious elegance of Mr Cowper with his

47

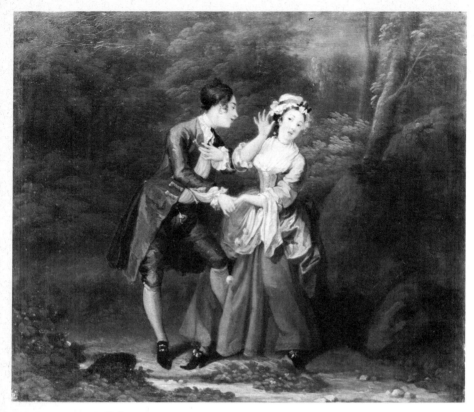

37 *Before*, 1730–31

greyhound, the exquisite, shimmering quality of Mrs Cowper's gown and
the sweet and artificial quality of the setting. A certain Watteau-esque
wistfulness may also be observed in the two paintings of *The House of Cards*,
and indeed a painting by C. A. Coypel (1694–1752) of children playing with
a house of cards could have been known to Hogarth through engravings.

One must look to France also for both versions of *Before* and *After*, one
set of which takes place indoors (Getty Museum, Malibu) and the other
outdoors (Fitzwilliam Museum, Cambridge). Hogarth may have had in
mind the well-established genre of French erotic book illustration, and it is
hard to resist the conclusion that in the Fitzwilliam paintings he has with
satirical intent set about to provide a down-to-earth English version of the
theme of pastoral courtship. The colouring is essentially pastoral, but the

30, 31

32, 33
37, 38

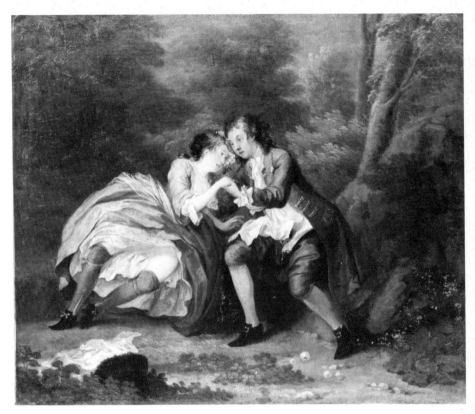

38   *After*, 1730–31

realistic depiction of the post-coital state undermines the distancing effect
of the pastoral convention. The underlying theme then is the contrast
between illusion and reality; the world of erotic delight offered by the
swain and the messy reality and bewilderment which follows what we are
meant to understand as a first attempt by both parties.

The overtly erotic nature of these cabinet paintings prompts one to ask
what sort of person bought paintings from Hogarth. To answer this we
need to look at an earlier and more sober painting of a Parliamentary
Committee. Probably through Thornhill, who was a Member of Parlia-   *40*
ment, Hogarth received permission to paint the Parliamentary Inquiry into
the Fleet and other prisons, the chief object of which was the appalling
régime of Warden Thomas Bambridge. Hogarth may have initially hoped

49

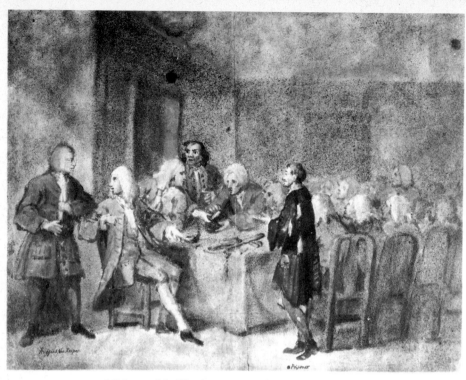

39　*A Prisoner of the Fleet being examined*, 1729

to cash in on the sensational nature of the accusations, for Bambridge was guilty of hideous cruelty in exacting money from his prisoners, and in
39　Hogarth's sketch (Fitzwilliam Museum, Cambridge) he is shown being accused by a ragged prisoner before the Committee headed by James
40　Oglethorpe. In the final picture (National Portrait Gallery) the need to produce portraits of the dozen or so members of the Committee has neutralized the drama, and Bambridge is shown revealing his vicious nature more obviously. The moral issue might have seemed straightforward – a cruel tyrant exposed by the assiduity of responsible citizens – but in retrospect the case is more equivocal. Until August 1728 the owner of the
41　patent for the Fleet Prison was John Huggins, who had the right to collect 'garnish' or fees from the inmates. Huggins's régime was notorious for extortion and rapaciousness, and it is likely that the rumbles of protest from those who had suffered his depredations made him part with the patent. He sold it to his deputy, the notorious Bambridge, who overstepped

50

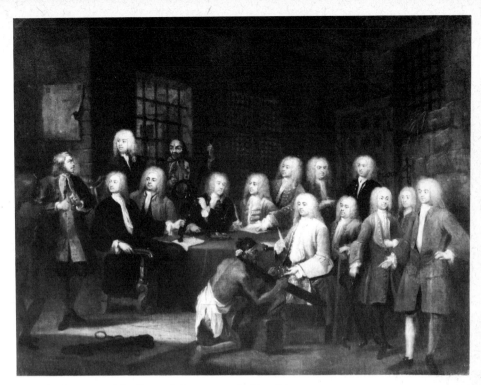

40   *The Committee of the House of Commons on the Fleet Prison*, 1729

the mark by his sadistic treatment of a well-connected architect and a baro-
net. Huggins was a friend of Thornhill, and commissioned work from him,
and he and his dilettante son William were to become close friends of
Hogarth, who painted two superb portraits of them. Huggins denied all   *41*
knowledge of the cruelties committed by his subordinate, and was exoner-
ated no doubt because of his social standing; one wonders whether Hogarth's
painting, which makes of Bambridge an almost mythological monster of
cruelty, was not inspired by the elder Huggins's side of the story, for after
the first owner Sir Archibald Grant became bankrupt in 1732, William
Huggins bought it, along with the Tate version of *The Beggar's Opera*.

It is noteworthy that a number of Hogarth's patrons at the time for both
conversation and other pictures were members of the Oglethorpe Committee, which suggests that Hogarth used the opportunity of Thornhill's
introduction to the full. Not surprisingly, perhaps, some of these men were
no more worthy than Huggins. John Thomson, who bought the outdoor

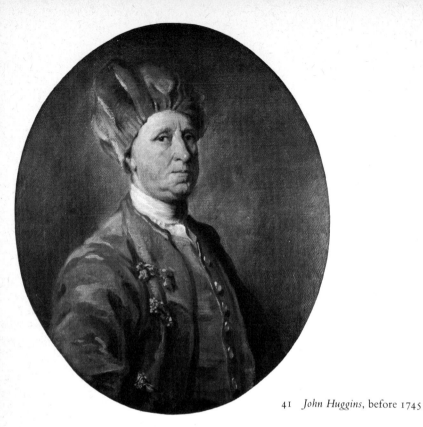

41 *John Huggins*, before 1745

37, 38   version of *Before* and *After*, absconded to France in 1731 after a financial scandal in which Sir Archibald Grant was also implicated and disgraced, involving the Charitable Corporation for the Relief of the Industrious Poor, whose funds they embezzled. George, Viscount Malpas, son-in-law

29   of the Prime Minister Sir Robert Walpole and later Earl of Cholmondeley, was another member of the Committee who became a patron of Hogarth, and no doubt others would prove to have been if we had more information about the provenance of some of the paintings. Another source of patronage would have come through Thomas Rich, who in addition to buying two

24   versions of *The Beggar's Opera* also commissioned a lost group of his family. Rich's friend the auctioneer Christopher Cock seems to have been the intermediary with Sir Andrew Fountaine, his father-in-law and Vice-Chamberlain to the Queen, who commissioned a portrait group. Hogarth even received a major commission from the financier and great Palladian supporter Sir Richard Child, for a large group seated in his Palladian Wanstead House (Philadelphia Museum of Art).

52

Hogarth's network of patrons thus covered the theatre and the worlds of the wealthy and socially prominent, and Vertue tells us that he also managed to sell some pictures, including *The Christening*, through a public sale in his studio in Covent Garden Piazza, which he had made something of a gathering place in its own right, by giving the impression that something scandalous and diverting could always be seen there. Vertue tells the story of the painting of Sir Isaac Shard, a notoriously harsh magistrate, whom Hogarth depicted sentencing a dog, which had stolen a shoulder of mutton, to death: 'numbers of people went to see [it] at the Painters & were mightily delighted with it', until in the end the victim's outraged son came to the studio and cut out his father's head from the painting. 25

Hogarth must have thrived on being such a sensation, and he clearly revelled in the company of frank-speaking and hedonistic gentlemen, but there were problems: he was attracting the patrons, but he was finding that conversation pictures did not properly repay the labour they took, so he sought a new field of activity. As he phrased it laconically in his *Autobiographical Notes*,

it had some novelty [and] succeeded for a few years . . . but . . . that manner of Painting was not sufficiently paid to do every thing my family required I therefore recommend[ed] those who come to me for them to other Painters and turn[ed] my thoughts to still a more new way of proceeding, viz. painting and Engraving modern moral Subject[s] a Field unbroke up in any Country or any age.

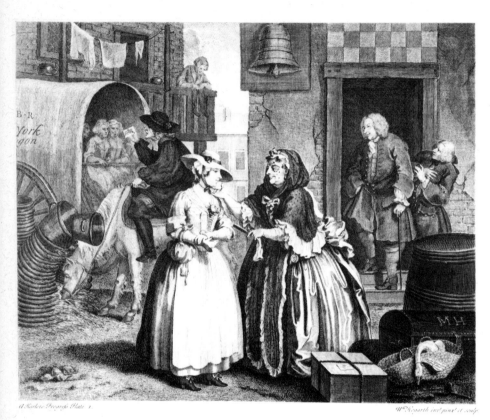

42 *A Harlot's Progress*, 1, engraving, 1731

CHAPTER THREE

Modern Moral Subjects: a Reading of the Two Progresses

HOGARTH'S PRIDE in his 'new way of proceeding' was justified by posterity, for it was his Modern Moral Subjects, or 'novels in paint', as they were often called, that were regarded in his own and the following century as his most important achievement, and led, for example, to William Hazlitt's claim that Hogarth was second only to Shakespeare as a student of the human comedy. By organizing pictorial images into series which tell a complete story of contemporary life Hogarth created a new kind of work of art. Like most plays of the period they have fully worked-out plots, dramatic confrontations and changes of scene, serious and tragic elements juxtaposed, and a high degree of topicality.

One can of course find precedents for many of these features in earlier pictorial art: Hogarth would have been familiar with painting cycles like Rubens' *History of Marie de Médicis* (Louvre, Paris), or for that matter Thornhill's cycle on the life of St Paul in St Paul's Cathedral. He certainly would have known the popular moralizing prints produced in Italy in the seventeenth century, which tell their story in the manner of a strip cartoon. He would have known Dutch paintings which take a moralizing view of contemporary life, and he must have seen a number of French paintings or engravings which depict contemporary manners with wit and subtlety. All these elements and many more contribute to the language of the Modern Moral Subjects, but in the end it is the stage and to a lesser degree the English novel and verse-satire which offered him a living tradition uniting all these elements. Hogarth's later remarks on his art all confirm the importance of dramatic performance, the conventions of which he had absorbed into his pictorial method while working on *The Beggar's Opera* paintings.   *23, 24*

There is a primary sense, therefore, as Hazlitt pointed out, in which Hogarth's paintings have to be *read* rather than contemplated, and Hogarth talked of his repertory of observed attitude and gesture as a form of language which the painter acquires much as a writer might develop his powers of expression. For this reason the first approach to Hogarth's Modern Moral Subjects must be to consider the first two series, *A Harlot's Progress* of 1731,   *42–47* of which only the engravings survive, and *The Rake's Progress* of 1735 (Sir   *49–56* John Soane's Museum) as continuing narratives telling a story which would have been comprehensible to his contemporaries.

Vertue tells us that *A Harlot's Progress* began originally with a single painting of an indecent nature, of a Drury Lane prostitute getting out of bed at noon. The idea of making it part of a series seems to have emerged in discussion in Hogarth's studio, among the group of cronies who bought some of his other subject paintings, and it is clear from Vertue's account that the initial impulse in making the series was not particularly high-minded.

42   In the first plate we see a pretty but gawky country girl appraised with apparent affection by a respectably dressed elderly lady, whom some contemporaries, including Vertue, recognized as the notorious bawd Mother Needham. The girl has just alighted from the York stage outside the Bell Inn in the City of London, and she is bound for her cousin, for whom she has brought a goose, which has round its neck a semi-literate message: 'For my Lofing Cosen in Tems Street in London'. The elderly gentleman in the doorway observing the scene was identified by Vertue as Colonel Charteris, a Don Juan whose powerful friends, according to general repute, saved him from hanging. In the background a country clergyman with a letter to the Bishop of London seeking preferment is oblivious to the moral danger faced by the country girl and the others still in the coach, and to the fact that his horse is toppling over a huge pile of pots and pans. This mishap introduces a note of impending catastrophe and may also refer to the danger to the girl's virginity. The goose she has brought her cousin may be an apt comment on her personality, and such details as the crumbling plaster also make comments on the instability of her situation, which at a moral level are easily stated: innocent country girls are easy prey to the powerful and unscrupulous and they can expect no guidance or charity in the big city. But Hogarth's attention is focused more fully on the vicious than on the innocent. The most powerful and intriguing figure is not the country girl but the magnificent figure of the bawd, whose Junoesque respectability is belied by the pock-marks on her face; yet something in the stance and gesture of both figures suggests a recognition by the bawd of her own youthful innocence. Indeed the whole work is full of such contrasts: between the youth and age of the two central figures; the respectability of the bawd's garments and her face; the gentlemanly bearing of Charteris and his lascivious leer. With this plate innocence takes its leave, and we are left entirely in the world governed by pimp and bawd.

43   In plate 2 Mary or Moll Hackabout (Hogarth only tells us she is M. Hackabout) is about to lose her position as the mistress of a wealthy Jew. Her progress to the eminence of a kept woman is not indicated by Hogarth, but was frequently charted without his authority in pornographic detail by later plagiarists, who reconstructed her path through employment and rape by Colonel Charteris, his rejection of her, her setting up with the Jew

56

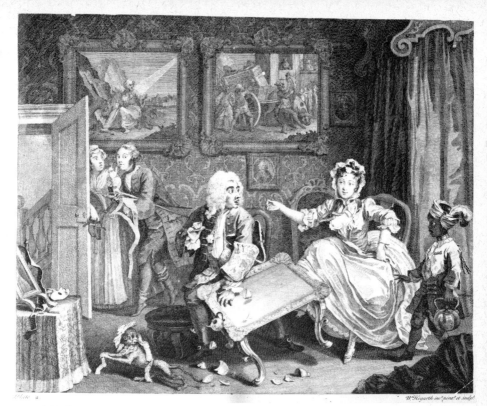

43　*A Harlot's Progress*, 2, engraving, 1731

in fine surroundings, until boredom was rapidly followed by infidelity. She
is seen making her lover's exit possible by snapping her fingers at her
protector and upsetting the tea table. The lover meanwhile, not quite
dressed, slips out past an astonished maid. The setting reveals her character
as a kept woman to be very different from the innocent country girl, and it
also hints at her future fate. Her pretensions to wealth and gentility are
shown by the keeping of a black houseboy and a pet monkey, and the
elegance with which tea is served. She apes the manners of a courtesan, but
her protector is not a courtier and her position, like the cups on the table,
is fragile. Her love of dalliance and taste for masquerades, evinced by the
mask on her dressing table, has overcome her prudence, and the breaking
of the crockery, as in the previous plate, is a harbinger of further catastrophe.

　　The next plate shows her still cheerful and feckless, but now lower on the
social scale, as a Covent Garden street prostitute. The previous plate can be
seen as expressing the shattering of her fantasy life, but up to that moment it
had some substance, for she was wealthy and had a young lover. Now the

44

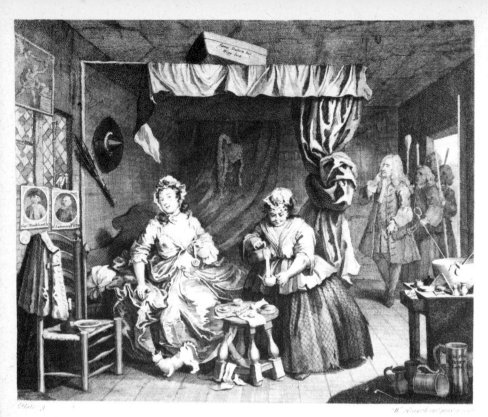

44   *A Harlot's Progress*, 3, engraving, 1731

gap has widened and her life is revealed as one of extreme squalor, balanced
by the romance of an affair with the dashing but doomed highwayman,
James Dalton, whose wig box rests on top of her bed, and the image of the
fictional Macheath whose print she has next to her bed. Instead of a black
houseboy in a turban she is attended by a hideously poxed bunter, and her
deceitful nature has descended to the open theft of a watch. Evidence of
revelry in the form of a chipped punchbowl, mugs and pipes lies in the
corner. The scene is also a point of transition for, squalid though her life is,
she has at least some independence, which she is on the point of losing to
the infamous Sir John Gonson, the scourge of harlots, who leads the heavily
armed watch to take her away. Sir John as he enters appears to hesitate as
if caught by lust at the sight of the Harlot's seductive presence, for it was an
old saw that such moralizing zeal was essentially prurient. The Harlot is also
seen as a religious dabbler, admiring the contentious divine Dr Sacheverell
and hanging near his portrait a eucharistic wafer. She wraps her butter in a

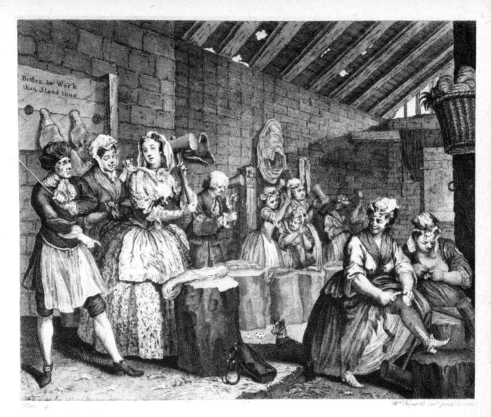

Better to Work
than Stand thus

45   *A Harlot's Progress*, 4, engraving, 1731

pastoral letter from the Bishop of London, which perhaps implies that
religious controversy is a danger to simple minds.

In the fourth plate she is now in Bridewell, the house of correction, where,   45
dressed in the finery of her former days, she is forced under threat of dire
punishment to beat hemp alongside the other inhabitants who are all
prostitutes, except for the pathetic gambler who has also lost all his worldly
possessions to his vice. Hemp was beaten to make rope, and its most sinister
function is referred to in a childish caricature on the back wall, of a hanging
man representing Sir John Gonson. The Harlot is still attractive and well-
dressed, but her future is represented by the hideous harlot behind who
fingers her garments and grins. The bunter ties up stockings which are
elegant but holed, exemplifying the decay of cloth and flesh equally.

In the fifth plate we leap straight to the Harlot's death in her own   46
premises. In a horrific scene she dies attended by her bunter, who looks in
shock at the doctors, identifiable as the infamous doctors Rock and

59

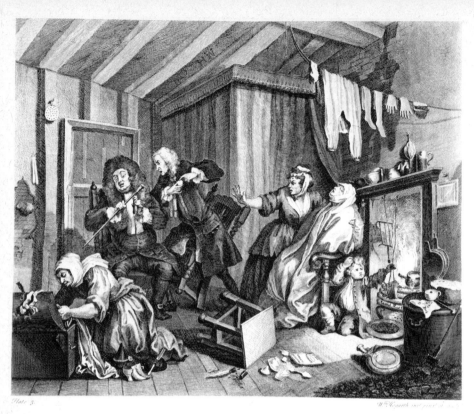

46   *A Harlot's Progress*, 5, engraving, 1731

Misaubin, quarrelling over the efficacy of their pills while their patient draws her last breath. Nowhere in Hogarth are comedy and tragedy so closely interwoven. The Harlot's gullibility about religion alluded to in

44   plate 3 is extended here to embrace quackery; the floor and surfaces are littered with evidence of her addiction to popular remedies for venereal disease. She has just had her teeth pulled by Dr Rock as part of a cure, but another woman has already prejudged the outcome by sorting out grave-clothes from a chest, which contains only masquerade garments. A new element is the introduction of a child who makes, somewhat belatedly, his first appearance. He is baffled by a piece of meat cooking on the fire, upon which a pot spills over and catches light. This sad episode alludes perhaps to his lack of upbringing, and the transmission of the sins and neglect of the parent.

47   The final scene is one of mourning over the coffin of Hackabout, who according to the plate on her coffin died on 2 September 1731 at the age of

60

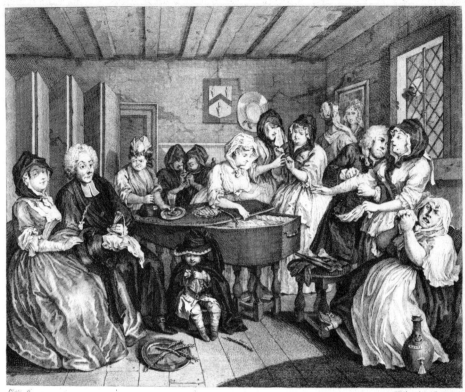

Plate 6.

47   *A Harlot's Progress*, 6, engraving, 1731

23. None of the mourners, except possibly one, is showing any sympathetic concern with the deceased, and we are presented with a spectrum of selfishness in the face of death. The parson is so preoccupied with surreptitiously feeling his willing companion that he spills his drink. The bunter to his left, the only person in the scene to have acted with human sympathy, looks on in disgust. Opposite them an elderly bawd, who may be Mother Needham lamenting the loss of revenue, wrings her hands in an exaggeratedly fervent manner, like a figure from a Baroque altarpiece. The only one who might be saved is the harlot who looks at the face of Hackabout in the coffin; the gesture of her hand suggests that she has realized from the corpse her own ultimate fate. The child in full mourning robes sits playing with a top before the coffin, not heeding the occasion or being heeded by anyone else. In this ghastly parody of a Lamentation group the only serious emotion is provoked by brandy ('Nants') and tears are shed not over death but over a cut finger.

From this reading a number of preliminary observations may be made. In the first place the subjects are relentlessly topical, addressing themselves without inhibition to contemporary life. Though we may see the characters as 'players in a dumb show', to use Hogarth's words, the acting is not simply tragic or comic, or even predominantly one or the other. The professions are satirized, but the humour evoked by their description is balanced by a genuine sense of horror at the fate of prostitutes. The humour is thus not detached from the tragedy; the quarrel of Misaubin and Rock at the death of the Harlot achieves its edge because of its tragic implications, and the presence of death brings to the surface the mordant humour of the final plate. *A Harlot's Progress* contains elements which could appeal equally to the parson and the hedonist, and it is not surprising that the engravings were an instant success with all classes of society.

The piracies which followed the publication of *A Harlot's Progress* were the tribute of Grub Street to its success. But to Hogarth they were also a threat to his rightful profits. He determined, therefore, to seek legal protection for any future publications. This he achieved with the aid of influential friends, by piloting through Parliament an Act to protect for the first time the copyright of engravers. The Act (later known as 'Hogarth's Act') became law on 25 June 1735, so he delayed publication of *The Rake's Progress* until that date, although he had announced the subscription for the plates late in 1733, and had finished the paintings by mid-1734. Here we are fortunate in having not only the original paintings (in Sir John Soane's Museum) but an oil sketch which probably represents an early idea for the series (Ashmolean Museum, Oxford). Hogarth conceived *The Rake's Progress* as an exploration of the polite world, as opposed to the sordid life of the Harlot. If she could appear as a hapless victim of exploitation, Hogarth allows the Rake no such excuse, except insofar as his spendthrift character can be blamed upon his miserly father. In the Ashmolean oil-sketch the Rake presides over every kind of aristocratic vice. He appears at the point of being married to an ugly spinster, from which business he is deflected by his jockey. In the foreground there are fake Roman busts bought at auction, and a painting, *The Rape of Ganymede*, perhaps as in *Marriage-a-la-Mode* alluding to homosexuality. In imitation of a gentleman who has been to Italy on the Grand Tour the Rake collects Old Master paintings, and Hogarth seems also to be implying that such a taste was a sign of susceptibility to Catholicism. The painting above the Rake's head is a bizarre parody of a Renaissance or Baroque altarpiece, in which the Madonna places the Child in a gigantic grinder which discharges gold coins for a priest to distribute to grovelling worshippers. Hangers-on, including a Grub Street poet, attend the Rake in an ante-chamber.

62

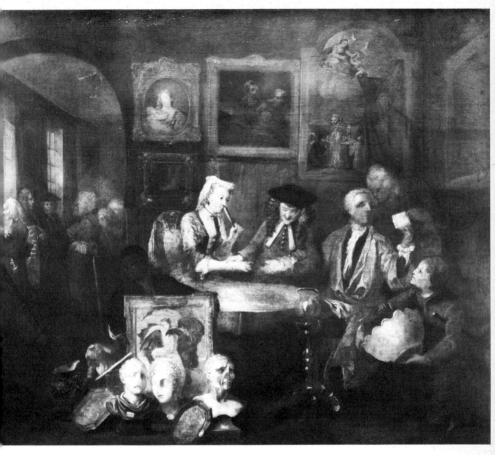

48   *The Marriage Contract, c.* 1732

The Ashmolean sketch contains in embryo many of the main themes of *The Rake's Progress*, especially the danger of seeking social success at the expense of moral integrity. In the final series some of these themes are separated out and become paintings in their own right, while others are dropped altogether. The episode with the jockey is absorbed into the Rake's Levée, and the marriage to the spinster takes place later as the Rake   50 tries to recoup his debts. The references to Papism and possibly homosexu-   53 ality, however, were eliminated and do not return, except incidentally in the case of the former.

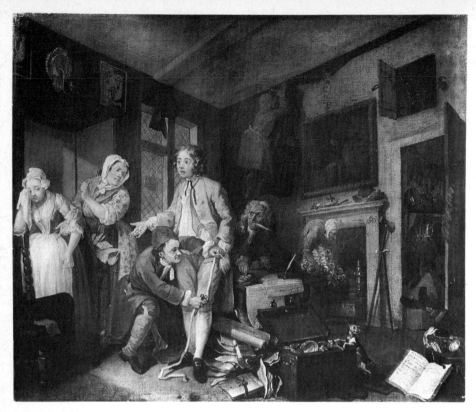

49 *The Rake's Progress*, 1: the Young Heir taking possession, 1733–34

The tragedy of the Rake follows from the fact that he is the son of a
miser: in the world of poetry and drama miserliness begets its contrary.
This bond between miser and spendthrift is affirmed by the name they
49 share, Rakewell, for the father is seen in the painting above the mantelpiece
raking in gold. There is an irony in the way in which the slow accumulation
of wealth is contrasted with its speedy disbursement by the son, whose
instinct is to buy his way in and out of every situation. The first picture
defines amply the characters of father and son and sows the seeds of future
disaster; at the same time the legal profession is thoroughly anatomized,
for the lawyer stealing the change is presumably also the author of all the
legal documents which litter the floor, and which contributed to the miser's
and his own wealth.
50 In the second scene the Rake is now established in London, and Hogarth
uses the device, familiar from dramatic comedy, of a morning levée to

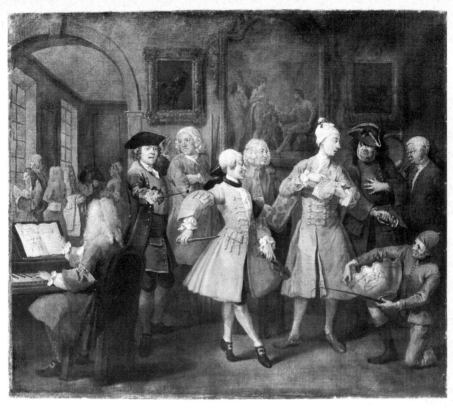

50   *The Rake's Progress*, 2: the Rake's Levée, 1733–34

draw together all the providers of costly and unnecessary services who encourage the Rake to ape the manners of the aristocracy. The Rake is besieged by a splendid group of grotesques, and we can assume that he falls for all their offers. The scene confirms his gullibility, but the real target lies in the panorama of the foolish extravagances of the *haut monde*; Rakewell by aspiring to them reveals their essential emptiness. The purveyors of false aristocratic culture are also satirized: foreign musicians are represented by the Handelian composer playing the music from his new opera *The Rape of the Sabines*. In the engraving a print on the floor alludes to the famous singer Farinelli, whose intoxicating style led a lady in the audience to cry out 'One God one Farinelli' and who attracted expensive gifts from the cognoscenti, including here Rakewell himself; French dancing masters, and indeed foreigners of every kind, are butts of Hogarth's wit. Some of the jokes are wonderfully schoolboyish: the ravishers in *The*

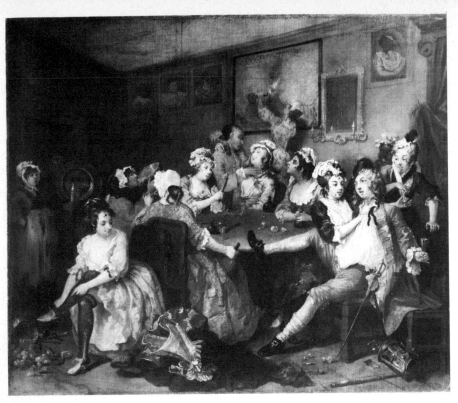

51   *The Rake's Progress*, 3: the Tavern Scene, 1733–34

Rape of the Sabines, in the cast-list added to the musician's keyboard in the
print, are all sung by well-known Italian eunuchs. The Rake's gullibility
shows him to be more fool than knave, but such foolishness leads quickly
to knavery.

51   In the Tavern Scene we see the sordid end to a night of brutal carousing,
in which a street fight with the watch has been followed by an early morning visit to a notorious brothel, the Rose Tavern in Covent Garden. The air
of ribaldry is so compelling, and the actuality of such incidents as the
prostitute spitting across the table is so palpable, that one might feel that
Hogarth is encouraging us to share the fun, but it would be wrong to
suggest that we are really meant to sympathize with the Rake. The super-
ficial gaiety is all shown to be sordid and ephemeral. The emblematic details
are full of disgust, from the chamberpot on the far left disgorging its
contents over a dish of roast chicken, to the row of portraits of Roman

66

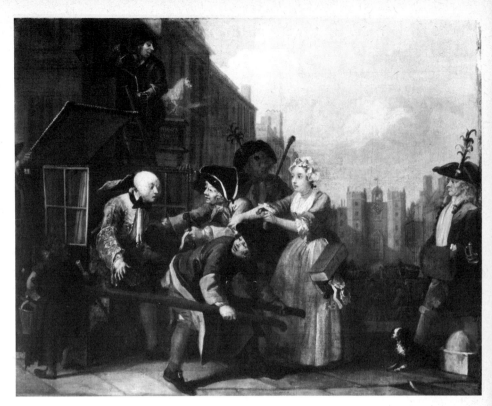

52   *The Rake's Progress*, 4: Arrested for Debt, 1733–34

emperors in which only Nero is not defaced. The 'posture woman' in the foreground is preparing for an obscene dance on a silver plate which will culminate in her extinguishing the candle in her vagina, and a ballad singer in the doorway holds 'The Black Joke', a notoriously obscene song. It is true that there is little hint here of Swiftian sexual disgust, but equally Hogarth makes it clear that the pleasures of the brothel are not deep or lasting.

A box of pills on the floor beneath the Rake suggests that he has already caught syphilis, but nonetheless he has had more opportunity than the Harlot to explore the world of pleasure. For the Rake illusion only gives way in the fourth scene. On the way to seek preferment at the Court of St   *52, 61* James, as he reaches towards the prize of being a courtier, the reality of his true financial position catches up with him: he is arrested for debt, and is just saved from prison by the ever loyal Sarah Young, who pays off his

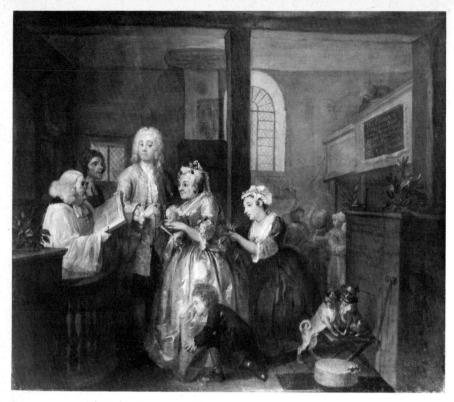

53 *The Rake's Progress*, 5: Marriage, 1733–34

creditors though only a poor seamstress. He will now be forced to make
money by whatever desperate expedient comes to hand. The gap between
reality and fantasy can only widen and reach its logical end in madness,
unless he renounces his foolishness and returns to his natural place by
redeeming his former fiancée. But he again chooses money rather than love
53   and marries a one-eyed elderly hunchback in order to retrieve his fortune.
The point of the Marriage Scene in the church of St Mary-le-Bone lies in the
implied alternative, which is repentance and a happy ending in the arms of
Sarah Young, who is seen in the background with her mother and baby
attempting to force her way into the church. (The resemblance to her of
the bridesmaid being ogled by the husband is accidental.) The clergy are no
help, for the church, despite recent 'beautification', is visibly decaying and
there is a significant crack through the Ten Commandments on the wall
behind the parson. The poorbox with cobwebs over it, on the far right,
evinces the lack of charity and the parson himself is a lascivious grotesque.

68

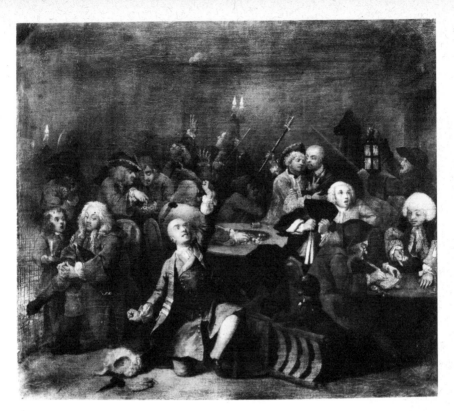

54 *The Rake's Progress*, 6: in a Gaming House, 1733–34

The marriage of convenience confirms rather than cures Rakewell's spendthrift nature, leaving gambling as the only way to recoup his fortunes. The Rake's imprecation to the Deity in the sixth painting achieves its 54 power through the unmistakable signs of madness in his physiognomy, noticed only by the boy bringing a drink to a miserable highwayman. The tragic shift in the Rake's personality is set against a spectrum of the miseries induced by gambling, the common denominator of which is total obsession, leaving the gamblers unaware of the fire breaking out in the wainscoting. Gambling, of course, cannot pay in a work of morality, and in the penulti- mate painting the Rake's mind has become wholly detached from reality 55 and he is now in the debtors' prison. He is beyond either comfort or entreaty now, and his condition has caused the still loyal Sarah Young to collapse in a faint. Reality is represented by his haranguing wife, the turnkey demanding 'garnish money', a boy demanding money for beer, and a terse rejection of a play the Rake has written from John Rich. But he is completely

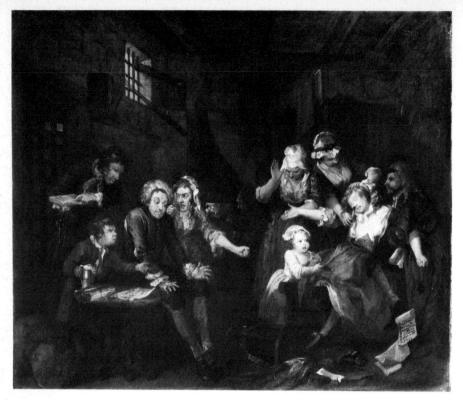

55   *The Rake's Progress*, 7: in the Debtors' Prison, 1733–34

unaware of them and his mind dwells in fantasy, represented by the wings
on the top of the four-poster bed, the alchemical experiments in the background, the telescope pointing to the heavens through the bars of his cell,
and a 'philosophical' book on the shelf next to some mortars. He is rapidly
approaching the pathetic condition of his cellmate, whose disordered mind
has given birth to the ultimate lunacy: a 'New Scheme for paying ye Debts
of ye Nation'.

   With madness firmly established there can be no other destination than
56 Bedlam: the final plate shows the Rake firmly in the grip of Melancholy
Madness, and we can, in the words of the verse text beneath the engraved
version, 'Behold Death grappling with Despair'. This death scene is one of
unequalled poignancy; Sarah Young mourns the Rake like Mary Magdalen
and the guard releases his chains as if freeing him from the rack of this cruel
world. On the other hand the setting is as richly comic as the Rake's death

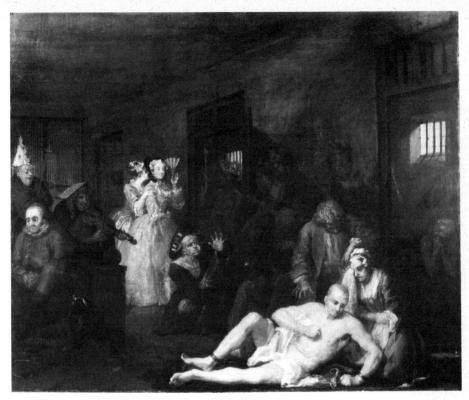

56   *The Rake's Progress*, 8: Bedlam, 1733–34

is tragic. The forms of madness are treated essentially as comments on the follies of the world, an idea strengthened when Hogarth returned to the plate in 1763 and placed a medallion of a demented Britannia on the wall. On the left of the print religious enthusiasm is represented by a madman striking the attitude of a hermit saint with prints of Clement, Athanasius and St Lawrence on the wall of his cell; a naked madman with a crown on his head, carrying a stick as a sceptre and urinating, is perhaps a blow against the Divine Right of kings; and the madman drawing elaborate trajectories in order to determine the longitude may be a reference to Nathanael Lee, a playwright who ended in Bedlam. Also within the confines of a madhouse are a well-dressed lady visitor and her maid; in the painting and the first state of the engraving the lady looks on in amusement at the man urinating, hypocritically shielding herself with a fan while the maid points gleefully. The Rake's last moments are of little interest to a world pursuing folly.

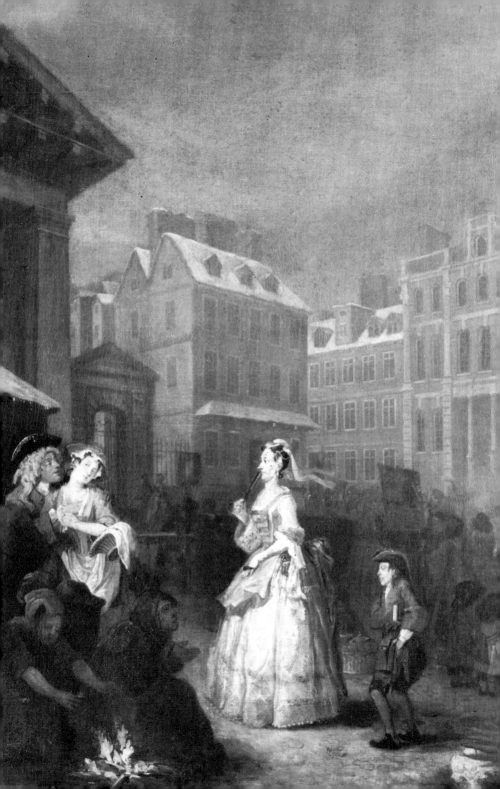

CHAPTER FOUR

The World of the Progresses

HOGARTH NO DOUBT HOPED that his painted series would last and be of interest to posterity, but his primary concern was to capture the interest of his contemporaries. He made no claims to universality except in the strictly moral sense, and the world of reference in his early paintings is confined to London, and indeed the London of coffee-houses, newspapers, City and Court. The reality or otherwise of Hogarth's characters can only be gauged, therefore, by looking at them in a well-defined context of time and place. On the other hand it must be remembered that the Progresses are as much works of fiction as any play or novel of the period; the reality we take for granted in Hogarth's paintings is no less a creation of his own mind than the historical setting of his Biblical and literary subjects. But then one could say precisely the same of Pope or Jonathan Swift, who frequently made real places and living people the subject of their poems. However there is more of a problem with painting for it does have, particularly in the hands of a master like Hogarth, the ability to persuade us that we are looking at a representation of real events, and that conviction can survive a full examination of the artifices used to achieve the final result.

We find, particularly in the eighteenth century, that the assumption is made almost universally that most of the characters in Hogarth had a real prototype, that each setting was precisely observed from a particular episode in his life, and one frequently encounters in memoirs and bio-graphies people who have claimed for instance to have witnessed the moment in the Tavern Scene in *The Rake's Progress* when one prostitute *51* spits in the other's eye across the table, or to have visited the very room in which the young couple are sitting in the second episode of *Marriage-a-la-* *80* *Mode*. Hogarth was aware from the beginning of his career as a painter that the public derived pleasure from seeing real people in paintings and prints, and that the rumour of such a thing could give a work instant popularity. A contemporary account of the reception of *Idleness and Industry*, possibly inspired by Hogarth himself, expresses the sense of wonder such recognition could cause among the audience who saw them in a print-shop window:

the first I heard break Silence was one of the Beadles belonging to the Court-End of the Town, who upon viewing the Print of the idle 'Prentice

73

at play in the Church-yard, breaks out with this Exclamation, addressed to a Companion he had along with him, G–d Z–ds, Dick, I'll be d–n'd if that is not Bob—, Beadle of St.— Parish; its as like him as one Herring is like another: see his Nose, his Chin, and the damn'd sour Look so natural to poor Bob.

Vertue also noted in his account of the genesis of *A Harlot's Progress* that Moll or Mary Hackabout was led astray by real people:

42   how this Girl came to Town. How Mother Needham. and Col. Charters [Charteris] first deluded her. how a Jew kept her how she livd in Drury lane. when she was sent to bridewell by Sr John Gonson Justice and her salivation [*sic*] & death.

Mother Needham, the celebrated bawd, after being pilloried, died on 2 May 1731, shortly before Hogarth began work on the series, and she was famous enough to be castigated both in Henry Fielding's *Covent Garden Tragedy* and in *The Dunciad*. Her special attribute was an affected piety which Fielding ridicules in the preface to his play: 'First, for the character of Mother Punchbowl; . . . From one line one might guess she was a bawd . . . but then, is she not continually talking of virtue? How can she be a bawd?' The man in the background, Colonel Charteris, as mentioned above, was equally notorious as an outrageous lecher and rapist who was more than once saved from the gallows by his wealth and powerful connections.

These two infamous characters appeared frequently in the scurrilous and satirical press and they were also the target of serious satirists who saw their vices as symptomatic of their age. That a bawd could pretend to piety and a rapist be a friend of the powerful and even be the subject, so Pope tells us, of a laudatory Grub Street biography, was indicative of the decadence of the times, which can no longer distinguish vice from virtue. The fact that Pope, Fielding and Hogarth chose the same targets reinforced their symbolic value, and gave them a mythical existence which transcended their real vices. The Orator Henley, for example, was satirized in *The Dunciad* not just as a figure of fun, but because his pretensions·to antique oratory and his claims as a primitive Christian were representative of the ignorance of so many preachers:

> Oh great Restorer of the good old Stage,
> Preacher at once, and Zany of thy Age!
> Oh worthy thou of Aegypt's wise abodes,
> A decent Priest, where monkeys were the Gods!
> But Fate with Butchers plac'd thy priestly Stall,
> Meek modern faith to murder, hack, and mawl.

Pope is true to the details of Henley's life, his preaching to butchers and even

74

his style of oratory, but in the last line he is elevated from a mere buffoon to a representative of the hypocritical enemies of faith. The print by Joseph Sympson after Hogarth's painting of *The Christening*, titled by the engraver *Orator Henley christening a Child*, on the other hand, converts him into a stock figure of the lecherous preacher, who neglects the business of baptism in order to ogle the females in attendance. He is a first cousin to the clerk eyeing the dozing girl in the *Sleeping Congregation* engraving.

Even where Hogarth refers to contemporary characters and events he employs a sensitivity fully attuned to pictorial modes and he also on occasion makes play with his characters' inability to distinguish fiction from reality. The Harlot has on the wall of her Drury Lane garret a print of Dr Sacheverell side by side with one of Captain Macheath, the hero of *The Beggar's Opera*, a fictional character – a joke both on her and on Dr Sacheverell. There can be no doubt that the Harlot and the Rake are themselves fictional, their personalities essentially stock properties of playwrights since the Restoration. They are less rounded than many of the other inhabitants of Hogarth's world, for their role is primarily to reveal and activate the vices of others. The Harlot by her ignorance falls into the hands of predators, but it is the mimicking of the vices of her protectors which makes her fall into perdition. The Rake's foolish desire for social position finds infinite encouragement in the world of fashion. He is in late seventeenth-century parlance a gull, a person of infinite credulity and cupidity, who can act as a foil or dupe of the vices of others by thinking only of today and not of tomorrow or the next world. He falls for the glossy surface presented by high society, and his total selfishness and lack of moral values do not allow him to see the sinful nature of the world of limitless pleasure.

If the Harlot and Rake are fictional this is not to say that they are unrelated to recognizable types of humanity. Nor does Hogarth intend his lawyers or doctors to be merely abstractions which stand for the predominant vices of their profession. They are meant to be convincing as real characters, yet have a universality which will touch and move the spectator. The issue was put succinctly by Fielding in *Joseph Andrews*, of 1742 (Book III, chap. I):

I question not but several of my readers will know the lawyer in the stage-coach the moment they hear his voice. It is likewise odds but the wit and the prude meet with some of their acquaintance, as well as all the rest of my characters. To prevent therefore any such malicious applications, I declare here once for all, I describe not men, but manners; not an individual, but a species. Perhaps it will be answered, Are not the characters then taken from life? To which I answer in the affirmative; nay I believe I might aver that I have writ little more than I have seen. The lawyer is not only alive, but hath been so these four thousand years . . .

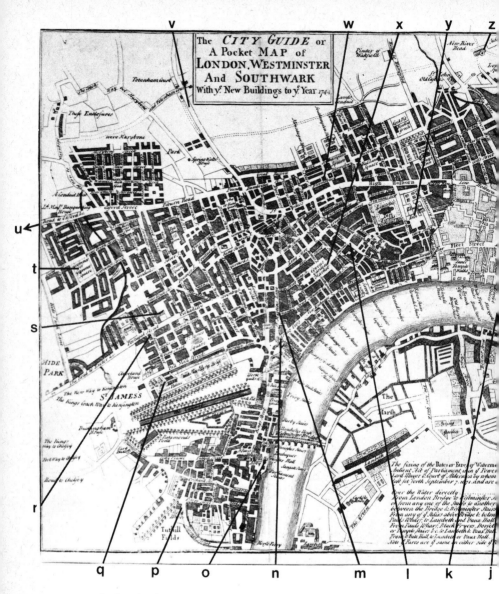

58   London in 1744.

The City and outlying parishes: a   St Bartholomew's Hospital; b   Grub Street;
c   Christ Church, Spitalfields; d   Bedlam; e   London Bridge; f   Guildhall;
g   Cheapside (Bell Inn); h   Newgate Prison; i   St Paul's; j   Fleet Prison;
k   Bridewell

Covent Garden and the West End: l   Drury Lane; m   St Martin's Lane;

76

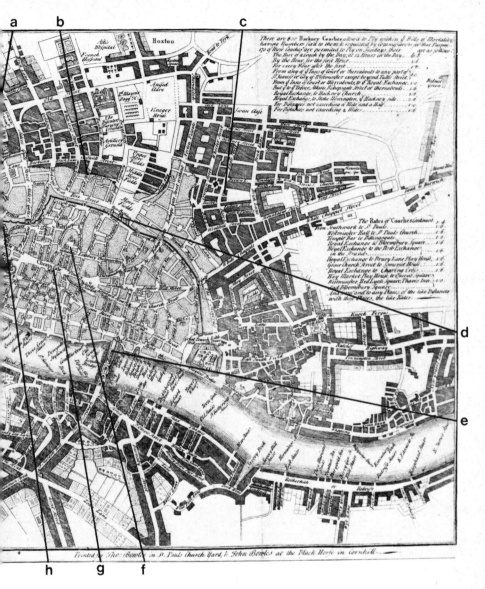

n Charing Cross; *o* Westminster Hall; *p* Tothill Fields Bridewell; *q* St James's Palace; *r* corner of Piccadilly and St James's Street; *s* Burlington House; *t* Grosvenor Square; *u* to Tyburn gibbet; *v* Tottenham Court Road (to Finchley); *w* St George's, Bloomsbury; *x* Covent Garden Piazza; *y* Lincoln's Inn

Northern suburbs: *z* Sadler's Wells

77

Paulson has observed that almost all the elements of the plot of *A Harlot's Progress* were available to Hogarth in the newspapers at the time when he was working on it. Colonel Charteris and Mother Needham were firm favourites of *The Grub Street Journal* and other scurrilous papers; and an oft-cited report described a prostitute sentenced to beat hemp in Bridewell, Tothill Fields, who was noted for the ladylike finery she wore when performing her tasks, a report surely echoed in the Bridewell scene in the *Harlot's Progress*.

45

Such actuality also extends to the setting in which the events take place, for one of the striking aspects of the Progresses and the moral series which followed is the precision with which the topography of London is brought into the action. Indeed it is this more than anything that separates Hogarth's moral series from previous strip cartoons or morality paintings, which tended to assert their universality by making the setting as featureless as possible. Like the characters the settings partake of fiction and reality, particularity and the universal. A building like the Fleet Prison had not only a real existence as a debtors' prison, but also a moral existence as the necessary fate of the spendthrift. Poets and satirists of the eighteenth century created a London of identifiable buildings and institutions which carried with them an implicit sense of moral imperatives. In the negative sense one thinks above all of the gibbet at Tyburn, the insane asylum of Bedlam and the house of correction in Bridewell, and on the positive side, although not always unequivocally, of the Guildhall, St Paul's Cathedral, and the Court of St James, all of which make their appearance in Hogarth's moral cycles.

139, 56

140
61

There is a sense, then, in which Hogarth meant the two Progresses to be a real journey as well. The Harlot and the Rake progress towards their latter end, but they also make a metaphorical progress through the streets and institutions of London. Behind Hogarth's titles for the series lie a number of different ideas. One thinks first of all of *The Pilgrim's Progress* (1678), the most widely available book in England after the Bible. Bunyan's Pilgrim's journey is internal and spiritual, taking place within the mind of the Christian wrestling with his conscience in a wicked world, but the primary metaphor of the book is a journey towards Jerusalem through a country in which different places, their inhabitants and natural features, stand for moral turning-points: the City of Destruction, the Slough of Despond, Village Morality, the Interpreter's House, the Hill Difficulty, and so on, all of which the Christian must pass through before he is vouchsafed a view of the Celestial City from the Delectable Mountains. Hogarth would have been aware of other kinds of progress in his daily life and these he would have shared with his fellow Londoners. The Lord Mayor's Procession on the day of his taking office, from the Guildhall in the City to

Westminster Hall, is one major example, and Aubrey Williams has argued that it is an important element in Pope's procession of the Dunces in *The Dunciad*, for which Pope may have considered the title 'The Progress of Dulness'. Another familiar progress which, like the Lord Mayor's Procession, is alluded to in a later moral series, was that of the condemned criminal, who made his final journey from Newgate Prison in the City to the gibbet at Tyburn, which stood in the open country not far from the grand squares of the aristocracy in the upper end of Westminster (near the present Marble Arch). On the eight hanging-days of the year the condemned were taken in a cart along the pre-ordained route through Holborn to what is now Oxford Street, thronged by crowds all the way; the procession made ritual stops at certain places, leading a contemporary to compare them to the Stations of the Cross on the way to Calvary. 140 139

Hogarth's Progresses in effect draw together the moral and physical ideas of the progress: the moral journey of the soul towards salvation or perdition, and the geographical progress through London. On the one hand there is the London of the great institutions, on the other the London of the parishes, the City and the West End, all of which have their allegorical value. In Hogarth's day London divided itself rather untidily into the City in the east with its parishes outside the walls, and Westminster to the west. The City had been largely destroyed and rebuilt after the Great Fire of 1666, and, partly as a consequence, men of wealth and social position, usually from the landed aristocracy, moved well beyond its western bounds. They set themselves up in grand spacious and well-ordered squares, which made a deliberate contrast with the winding alleys and picturesque courtyards of the older parts of London. This division of London into City and West End became clarified towards the end of the seventeenth century, a great age of speculative building. The difference in architecture, between the slightly crude, rather unsophisticated pomp of the public buildings in the City and the elegant and learned Palladianism of the West End, clearly reflected (as John Summerson noted) a difference in ethos. By Hogarth's day the ways of life of the two cities had been codified in literature into the contrasting types of merchant and aristocratic fop. 58 59

Hogarth was to explore this double distinction in the *Marriage-a-la-Mode* series, in the personalities of the Merchant and the Earl. Lord Squander's house, with its painted ceilings and mainly Italian Old Master paintings, can be placed in the West End. In seeking to keep up with his fellow aristocrats he has embarked upon the building of a vast Palladian mansion which can be seen through the window, and which has brought him to the indignity of having to sell his great name through his only son to a City merchant. The dénouement takes place in the house of the bride's father, 79 84

79

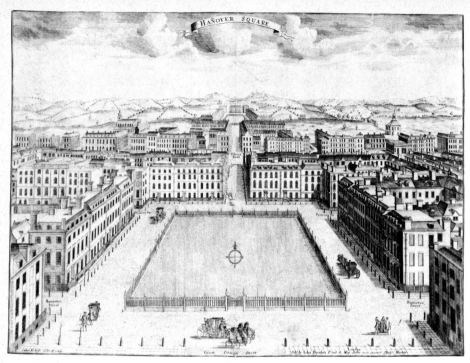

59 Hanover Square, laid out *c.* 1715

60   from the window of which old London Bridge can be seen, epitomizing
the ramshackle and disorderly visual spectacle the City must have presented
in this time. The merchant's house is plain, dark and mean, with bare floor-
boards and old-fashioned panelled walls which exhibit his 'low' taste for
Dutch paintings of boors.

    Both the Harlot and the Rake begin their careers in the City; the Harlot

42 descends from the York stage in Cheapside, while the Rake sets off on his
49 journey from a house which exhibits the same archaic miserliness as the
merchant's house in the *Marriage-a-la-Mode*. On the other hand the Rake
is able to explore the fleshpots of the polite world to the west of the City,
while the less fortunate Harlot probably does not reach beyond Covent

52 Garden; the Rake seeks a position at the Court of St James, while the high
point of the Harlot's life was to be the mistress of a Jew, who was, however,
rich, likely to be living either in the City or Covent Garden. Covent Garden,
where Hogarth himself lived, in Thornhill's house in the Piazza in the early
1730s, represented the meeting point between low life and the dissolute

80

                  60   Old London Bridge, from the window of the
merchant's house in the last scene of *Marriage-a-la-Mode*
(see ill. 84), 1743

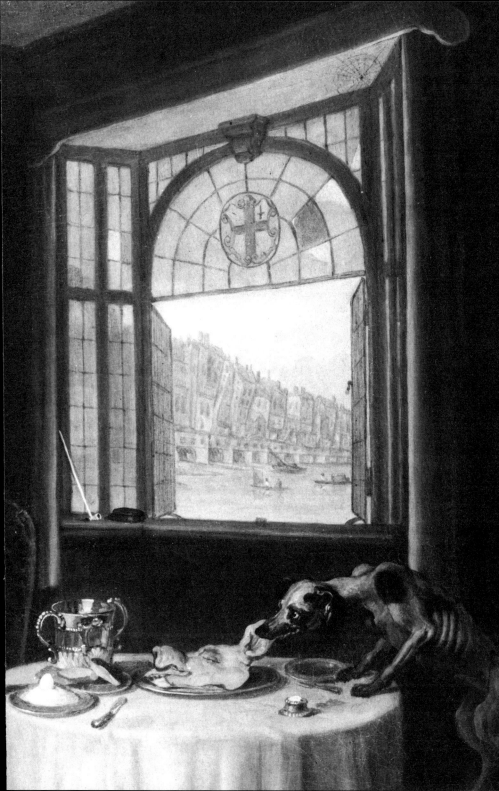

aristocracy. There were to be found the brothels, gambling dens, 'bagnios' or houses of assignation where masquerades might take place, theatres and shows of all kinds. If the Harlot and the Rake had met it would have been in Drury Lane, which accommodated both the Rose Tavern, where the Rake loses his watch, and the Harlot's lodgings, where she steals one. It is the realm of night which John Gay characterized as

> Drury's mazy Courts, and dark Abodes,
> The Harlots' guileful Paths, who nightly stand,
> Where Katherine-street descends into the Strand.

Covent Garden also had its respectable citizens, including large numbers of Huguenot immigrants and craftsmen, and much of the humour in the three paintings of the *Times of Day* series which are set in or near Covent Garden lies in their confrontation with the riff-raff who share it with them: the prude who looks sniffily at the uncouth customers of Tom King's Coffee House in the Piazza, and the Huguenot congregation whose Sunday-best and genteel manners contrast with the racy untidiness on the other side of the ditch.

The Rake reaches the West End in the second scene of his Progress, and his Levée represents the taste of the polite world of fashion, which gravitates around the environs of the Court. The West End, according to John Hoadly's words under the engraving of the Levée, is where

> Pleasure on her silver Throne
> Smiling comes, nor comes alone;
> Venus moves with her along:
> And smooth Lyoeus [Bacchus];
> And in their Train, to fill the Press,
> Come apish Dance, and swolen Excess,
> Mechanic Honour, vicious Taste,
> And fashion in her changing Vest.

The Rake reaches his nemesis as he is hauled from his coach in the queue for a grand reception at St James's Palace. He is arrested at a point still recognizable today, on the corner of Piccadilly looking down St James's, a few yards from Lord Burlington's great mansion, Burlington House. His marriage to the hunchback also gains added meaning from its setting, for it takes place in the church of St Mary-le-Bone, in a tiny village to the north of the great squares of the West End, now Marylebone, the distance from the town suggesting the furtive nature of the proceedings.

82

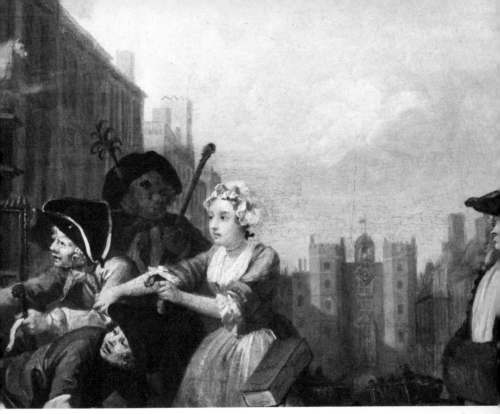

61   Looking from Piccadilly to St James's Palace: detail of scene 4 of *The Rake's Progress*, 1733–34 (see ill. 52)

The topographical setting of the Rake's end is more clearly defined than that of the Harlot. He progresses from a gambling den in Covent Garden to those two terrible institutions just outside the walls of the City, the Fleet Prison and Bedlam. She, on the other hand, passes to a bridewell, which could be the original one in Bridewell Palace near the Fleet Prison, or, as Paulson thinks, the Bridewell in Tothill Fields, west of Westminster. Her death may take place in Covent Garden, but she might equally have descended to one of the infamous lodging-houses in the parish of St Giles-in-the-Fields (near what is now New Oxford Street), which is also the setting of *Gin Lane*. On the whole, there is a greater sense of topographical precision in *The Rake's Progress*, and a greater sense of the satirical possibilities that lie in the places as well as the people of London, and this may be indicative of the richer vocabulary Hogarth was able to bring to his second series of Modern Moral Subjects.

55
56
45

46

144

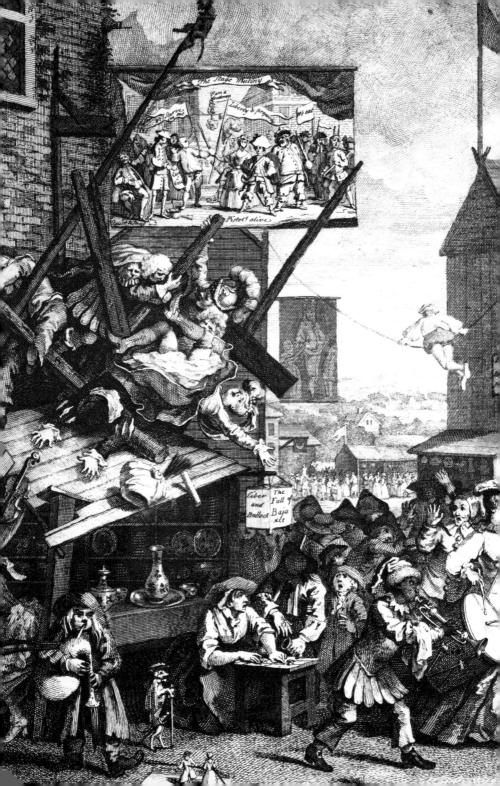

The Stage Mutiny

I am a Gentleman

Liberty & property

Poor R—ch

we eat

Pistol's alive

The Fall of Bajazet

Colour and Bullock

CHAPTER FIVE

The 1730s: Satire and History

THE SUCCESS of the Progresses was enough to establish Hogarth as one of the most notable men of his day in London, and he was able to profit from his achievement by creating his own market for his engravings. He never found it easy to sell the original paintings for the Modern Moral Subjects; his profits and reputation came entirely from the prints, the sale of which he managed to control, despite the activities of pirate publishers and printsellers. He achieved this on the whole by appealing to a public beyond the traditional picture and print market: his engravings were as far as we know popular with most classes of society, not excluding those who were satirized. For the first time serious works of art conceived and executed by an English artist were placed in the hands of a public who could not normally afford to buy original paintings.

Many of the purchasers were middle-class, and Hogarth has often been seen as representing aspirations quite different from those of the aristocratic élite who drew their culture from Italy and France. This is an over-simplified view, more true on some levels than others, for the broad process of social change does not always clarify the circumstances of an individual artist and his patrons. It is possible to argue, like Antal, that Hogarth was an essentially 'middle-class artist', the moral purpose of whose art 'had its origin in the new bourgeois outlook', but at the conscious level in the Progresses the merchant class are as much the butt of his satire as the aristocracy.

The one exception to this rule and the most positive endorsement of a bourgeois ethic in Hogarth's career is the *Industry and Idleness* series, which *134–140* charts the rise of an industrious apprentice through conformity and hard work to the office of Lord Mayor of London. This series, however, was made some fifteen years later than the Progresses, and, as we shall see, it owes its morality more to the consciously didactic ambience of the next decade, and the influence of George Lillo and the mature Henry Fielding. The Harlot's sin is not idleness specifically, but rather, like the Rake, to have aspired above her destined social class by mimicking the vices of her social superiors. In *The Rake's Progress* the process of destruction begins with the miserliness of the Rake's merchant father, whose diligent raking in of cash is seen as the primary cause of the Rake's spendthrift nature.

On the other hand one can connect Hogarth's broader concerns with the more pragmatic and rational culture of the early eighteenth century, in his belief in observation, his hatred of superstition which he extended to include Catholicism and any kind of Nonconformity, and his humanitarianism. Hogarth's instinctive reaction is to dismiss all metaphysics as 'mystery' or 'superstition', and in that sense he is a true citizen of the age of Locke. The Rake's punishment follows logically from his sins, and retribution is dealt to him in this world in just proportion.

To set Hogarth's beliefs into a wider context it is perhaps most useful to look at one of his closest friends. In some respects Benjamin Hoadly, Bishop of Winchester, was the archetypal worldly prelate, keeping a notably good table and holding the Bishopric of Bangor in Wales for six years without visiting his see once in that time. To some of his contemporaries he appeared as a contemptible toady, always ready to flatter the royal family for the sake of preferment. On the other hand he was a great controversialist and one of the strongest intellects in the Church of his day. He remained in high favour at Court without compromise to his Whig principles, and he argued fervently and openly against the divine authority of the King and his own Church. As a latitudinarian he was hostile to mystery and dogma, and in 1735 he published a pamphlet on the sacrament of the Last Supper which argued that it should be seen not as a mystery but only as a commemorative rite. He was actively opposed to Nonconformity and Catholicism, but notably tolerant of different beliefs within the Church of England. Hogarth's painting of *The Good Samaritan* for St Bartholomew's Hospital in London bears the marks of Hoadly's views on the supremacy of works over faith, and he would have been sympathetic to Hogarth's interest in charitable works, which emerged in the 1730s with the painter's growing connection with Bart's Hospital and the Foundling Hospital.

In the mid-1730s one can also see the growth of an artistic circle revolving around Hogarth, particularly in the art school in St Martin's Lane which he inherited from Thornhill, and ran on consciously free and democratic lines. Among the teachers were the French engraver Hubert Gravelot (1699–1773), the painter Frank Hayman (1708–76) and the sculptor Louis François Roubiliac (1702/05–62). The Hogarth circle was distinguished by informality of style, theatrical connections and, despite many of Hogarth's public pronouncements, a susceptibility to French influence. The effect of French prototypes on Hogarth's conversation groups has already been noted; after about 1735 a less definable but more pervasive Rococo feeling enters the work of the group, which culminated in the project for the decoration of the Vauxhall Pleasure Gardens owned by Hogarth's friend Jonathan Tyers. It is still debatable whether Hogarth actually made any paintings

86

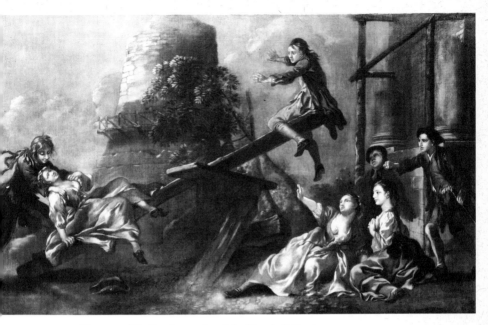

63   Francis Hayman: *The See-Saw*, painted for Vauxhall Gardens, *c.* 1740–43

directly for Vauxhall, although copies of some of his paintings did adorn
the supper boxes; in fact he seems to have kept a certain distance from it, but
the influence of the Gardens' informality and light-heartedness can be felt
in many of Hogarth's satirical paintings of the later 1730s.

The impact of the two Progresses was so great that one tends to forget
that at the same time Hogarth made satirical paintings of quite a different
character. *The Rake's Progress* was issued with an engraving of a painting
of *Southwark Fair*, which does not tell a narrative story and in that respect   64
foreshadows several which deal with human beings *en masse*. In these
paintings humanity is anatomized with close observation and humour, in all
its greed, selfishness and pursuit of pleasure, not through representative
types of sins and sinners, but through the interaction of groups and individuals. The theme and composition of *Southwark Fair* follow that of the
early print *Masquerades and Operas*, but the theme is broader in scope. The   9
central metaphor, an enduring one in Hogarth's work, is the domi-
nance in the affairs of men of illusion over reality; and we see the potential
collapse of that illusion in the fall of the flimsy stage on the left upon the   62
milling humanity beneath. The sense of the world given over to folly and

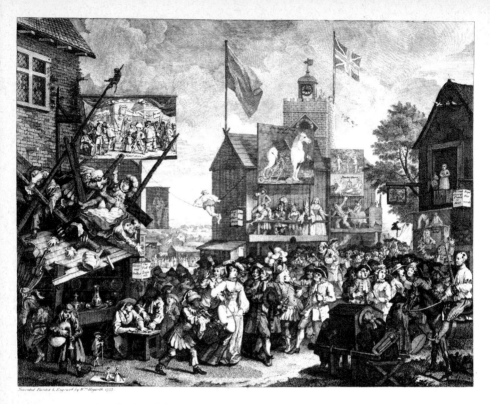

64   *Southwark Fair*, engraving, 1733

vice is conveyed by the way in which the church tower (religion) and the
flag (patriotism) are echoed and partly concealed by 'Lee & Harpers
Great Booth', which is showing *The Siege of Troy* and a Biblical travesty,
Jephthah's Rash Vow. The latter, as Paulson points out, was actually produced in 1733 and was a characteristic popular farrago of the period,
attaching to the Biblical story every kind of harlequinade and pantomime.
To the right the juxtaposition of a showcloth of *Adam and Eve* with one
below of *Punches Opera* showing 'Punch and Joan at Hellmouth', suggests
the trivialization of Original Sin; a rope-flyer leaping from the church
tower may parallel this fall, while also indicating that the church has become
merely an adjunct to a fairground act.

The topical references to known performers and plays show that one of
Hogarth's aims was, as he later claimed, to create works which 'may be
instructive to future time when the customs manners fasheons and humours

of the present age may [be] changed'. The moral intention of the painting is not immediately apparent, nor are the consequences of sin made as explicit as in the Progresses. The spectator's propensity to laugh at trivial entertainment should itself lead him towards enlightenment. This point is expressed in the inscription beneath another engraving, *A Midnight Modern Conversation*, where a warning is also given against seeing the protagonists as particular individuals:

> Think not to find one meant Resemblance there
> We lash the Vices but the Persons spare
> Prints should be prizd as Authors should be read
> Who sharply smile prevailing Folly dead.

We as spectators are intended to pass from reading the prints as satires of others to seeing ourselves in the follies depicted. *We* are the true objects of satire, and the vanity of the world is a product not of outside forces but of our own folly. Within the Swiftian idea, that the satirist should 'laugh mankind out of its favourite follies and vices', is a creative paradox: one panders to triviality in order to expose it.

Southwark Fair itself represents the logical conclusion of the contemporary trivialization of the stage: drama is now the barely-heeded entertainment of the mob, a condition to which its surrender to travesty and its neglect of its great traditions have led it. The play on the collapsing stage is appropriately *The Fall of Bajazet*, being performed by the company of Theophilus Cibber, which had in a recent *cause célèbre* withdrawn from the Drury Lane Theatre after a takeover by a rich dilettante, and, led by Cibber under the banner of 'liberty and property', had set up on its own (events depicted on the backcloth in the print). The collapse of the stage refers to Cibber's pretentions, the Cibber family being a favourite target of satirists; as the company tumble down their overblown historical costumes are disarrayed, allowing one of the actors a surreptitious peep up the skirts of an upturned actress. The fall to be enacted in the play thus becomes a physical fall, which is on the point of spreading further destruction: the falling stage will smash the china on the stall beneath, hit the gamblers arguing obliviously over dice and the dog dressed as a parading gentleman, and eventually engulf a part of the crowd. The action progresses from the petty quarrels of actors to their flimsy world of illusion, and then to the real consequences of their actions, which can cause destruction not only of illusions but of real people. Behind such imagery is the idea, dear to the satirists of the age, that the corruption of art was symptomatic of the corruption of society, and could bring about the latter by blurring the distinction between illusion and reality.

62

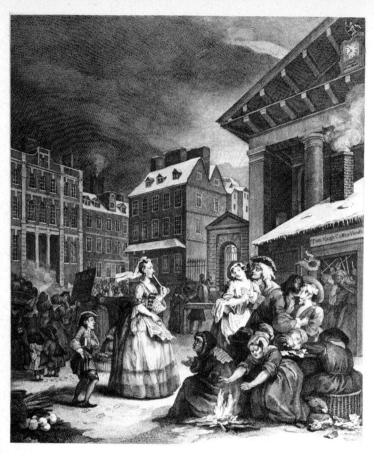

65 *Morning*,
engraving, 1738
(compare ill. 57)

For all its underlying satirical intent *Southwark Fair* is quite without the sense of tragedy of the two Progresses. Despite the scene in the foreground of the beautiful drummeress beset by an ugly and sordid crowd, there is no specific focus for the frenetic energy which rages through the work. The careful plotting of *The Rake's Progress* gives way here to a greater concern with humanity in action, represented not by individuals but by the crowd. In fact *The Rake's Progress* was not followed by another series of Modern Moral Subjects for nearly ten years, and Hogarth no doubt felt that his achievement of wealth and fame allowed him to try new modes and paint for his own pleasure. The four paintings of *The Times of Day* of 1738 (National Trust, Upton House; and Private Collection) show a greater concern with the comedy of daily life, and they are unified not by a coherent story but by contrasts of mood and incident. The diurnal cycle begins quietly in the morning, with the famous figure of the prude crossing

57, 65

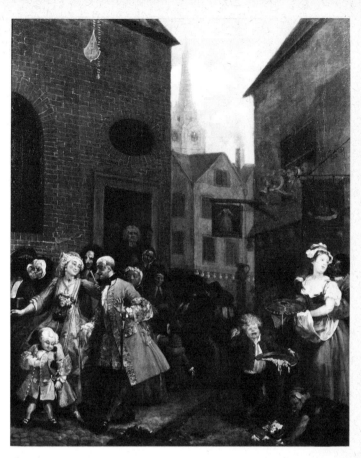

66 *Noon*, 1738

Covent Garden Piazza, disapproving of the amorous scenes outside the notorious Tom King's Coffee House. As a study of character she is, as Fielding recognized, one of Hogarth's supreme creations, for her chilly soul is given not only to prurience (cf. Sir John Gonson's arrest of the Harlot in *A Harlot's Progress*) but also to cruelty, indicated by the freezing little boy who carries her Bible. The contrast is between cold- and hot-blooded vices; the grand portico of St Paul's, Covent Garden, presides over the ephemeral pleasures of man, and dominates Tom King's Coffee House, which Hogarth has artfully shifted from its real place in the Piazza to make an ironical contrast with the church behind. In *Noon* the buildings are also artfully juxtaposed to make a contrast between the vices of order and disorder. A rowdy pub on one side, where greed and lust are rampant, is contrasted with the extreme formality of a Huguenot church on the other side, its congregation dressed soberly or with extreme foppishness. Neither is given moral

44

66

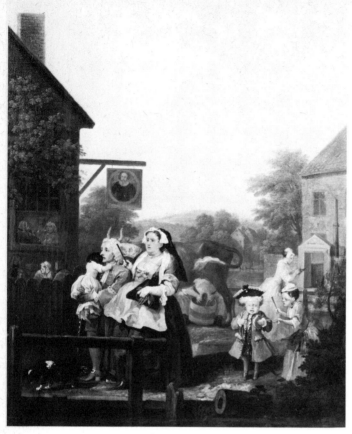

67   *Evening*, 1738

preference by Hogarth, and they are both symbolically distant from the noble spire of St Giles-in-the-Fields in the background. The chain of destruction in front of the pub begins with a lustful black grabbing the breasts of a serving maid, and ends with a child eating food that has spilled on to the

67 street. The main object of satire in *Evening* is the scolding woman whose dominant presence overwhelms the poor little dyer (identifiable by his blue hands) who carries the child. Hogarth indicates the shrew's lustfulness by her fan, which shows *Venus detaining Adonis from the Chase*, and the artfully placed cow's horns which indicate her husband's cuckoldry. As Paulson has pointed out, the theme is also of frustrated escape: the couple have gone to Sadler's Wells, a watering place just outside the City, but have failed to find either coolness or solace from each other, and their unhappiness is mirrored by the squabbling children behind them. In *Night* we return to the

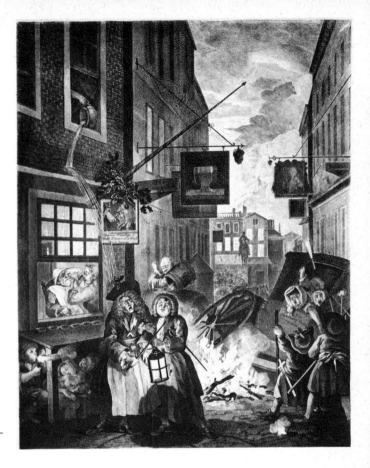

68 *Night*, engraving, 1738

horrors of low life in the town, where the statue of Charles I at Charing 68
Cross can be seen dimly presiding over a sordid street full of bagnios and
quacks, in which the watch makes only an ineffectual presence. An altogether sharper note of satire is struck in this final scene, for the accident to
the 'Salisbury Flying Coach' near a bonfire looks extremely threatening to
the passengers: a disastrous conclusion is made likely as always by the greed
and heedlessness of mankind. The imminence of destruction by fire is
taken up in the smoke clouds in the background hinting at an apocalyptic
conflagration, which recalls the fire in the gambling den in *The Rake's* 54
Progress, and may refer to the popular belief that the Great Fire of 1666 was
a manifestation of the wrath of God at the sins of Londoners. The imagery
of *Night* brings the cycle, which began with such gentle humour, to a
brutal end.

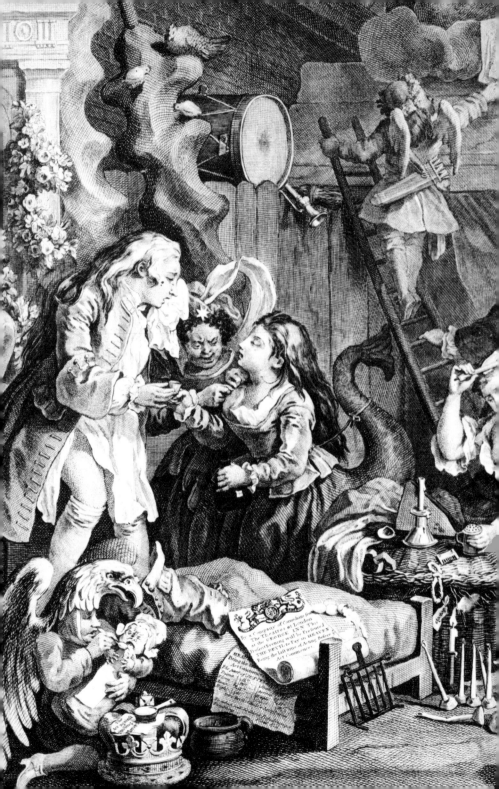

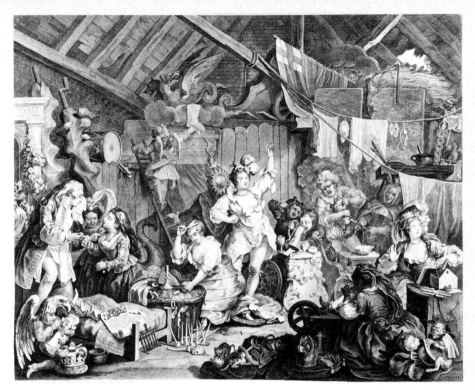

69, 70 *Strolling Actresses dressing in a Barn*, engraving, 1738

Strolling Actresses dressing in a Barn, an engraving for which the original 69, 70 painting was destroyed in the nineteenth century, was published later in 1738, and shows a greater concentration on a single idea which unites the diversity of human reaction. The theme, of actresses preparing for a country performance of a play in the humble and uncomfortable setting of a barn, lies in the contrast between the reality of life for the acting company and the illusion they present in the play. The result is more poignant and profound than anything Hogarth had done before, for it elevates this contrast to a sense of the vanity of earthly things. In the end it is not the stage which is being satirized but all human pretensions: in the foreground the kittens playing with the orb and the lyre invoke the world of the *memento mori*. The stage props lying around the barn have their functions ruthlessly inverted: a crown is used as a table for a baby's gruel and a classical altar as a table for beer and pipes, a cupid has hung his socks to dry on a dragon's cloud, and so on. These elements were the stock-in-trade of the allegorical wall-painter as well, and the design can also be seen as an affectionate parody of the kind of painting in which figures fly through the air carrying empty symbols of office.

The great satirical paintings of the 1730s represent only a part of Hogarth's activity in that decade. He began before 1735 to explore the possibilities of History painting, and in particular the depiction of subjects from the Bible. He gives a typically sardonic view of his first attempt in his *Autobiographical Notes*:

the puffing in books about the grand stile of history painting put him upon trying how that might take, so without haveing a stroke of this grand business before . . . he painted a great stair case at Bartholomews Hospital with two scripture-stories . . . this present to the charity he . . . thought might serve to shew that were there any inclination in England for Historical painting such a first essay whould Proove it more easily attainable than is imagined.

In fact he left out what was certainly the main reason, which was that Sir James Thornhill had died on 4 May 1734. Thornhill's office as Serjeant-Painter went to his indolent son John, but Hogarth may have seen an opportunity to take over his father-in-law's vacant office of painter to the royal family, and perhaps even had hopes of occupying his role as, in Vertue's words, 'the greatest History [painter] this Kingdom has produced'.

Vertue saw the influence of Kent in all the misfortunes that befell Thornhill in his later years, and forced him into virtual retirement with nothing to do but copy the Raphael Cartoons at Hampton Court (now in the Victoria and Albert Museum). The beginning of Thornhill's decline came as early as 1722, with Kent's success in wresting from him the commission to decorate the interior of Kensington Palace, and a decorative scheme for Moor Park had also ended disastrously in a law suit at the end of that decade. Vertue, who was not alone in seeing Kent's hand in this setback to Thornhill's reputation, commented:

Mr. Kents friends & interest no doubt endeavoured to foment this difference & slurr the reputation of Sr James. tho' it was the true opinion of the Several artists Judges in this case. that Sir James had excelld in this work. particularly as he designed it to Rival all his competitors. But what is Merit when envy joynd with power. to oppose it.

This question was no doubt on Hogarth's lips when in 1733 he was out-manoeuvred by Kent for the royal commission to paint the marriage of the Princess Royal. Again Vertue tells the story with convincing finality:

these are sad Mortifications to an Ingenious Man [Hogarth]. But its the effect
of carricatures wch he has heretofore toucht Mr Kent. and diverted the
Town [presumably a reference to *Masquerades and Operas*, but Kent might
also have believed the anonymous caricature entitled *Taste, or Burlington
Gate* was by Hogarth] which now he is like to pay for, when he least thought
of it. add to that there is some other causes relateng to Sir James Thornhill...

9

It must have been especially galling to Sir James to have lost the Moor
Park commission to Jacopo Amiconi (1675–1752), the Venetian painter,
when he had so successfully used his Englishness to snatch commissions

71

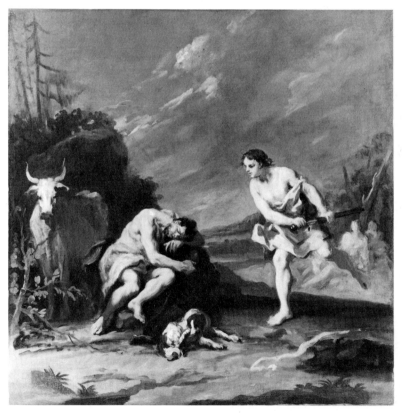

71 Jacopo Amiconi: *Mercury about to slay Argus*, sketch for a wall-painting at
Moor Park, 1730–32

from his French and Italian rivals. Amiconi was, however, a worthy opponent and his paintings at Moor Park have a lightness of touch and Rococo quality that made posterity if not Thornhill the richer. Amiconi would have been interesting to Hogarth in other respects. He was closely connected with the Italian opera, and was an intimate friend of the great singer Farinelli, whom Hogarth had already ridiculed in the Rake's Levée. Furthermore he had shown an excellent flair for the public gesture. Vertue tells of Amiconi's work for Lord Tankerville in 1731:

Signr Amiconi Painter when he had finisht the Stair at Lord Tankerfields St James's Square – his Lordship being well pleas'd desird to know what he must pay for it. Amiconi produc'd a bill of costs for Materials Scaffolds Colours &c. which amounted to £90 or thereabouts. which was all he requird and the favour & protection of the Lord. being otherwayes for his labour enough satisfyd to have the opportunity to show what he was capable of doing in so convenient a place – which was so modest & obliging. therefore that Nobleman immediately gave him a bank bill of two hundred pounds.

Hogarth must have been especially stung, therefore, when he heard that Amiconi was about to be offered the large commission for a major wall-painting to go in the entrance hall of the newly rebuilt St Bartholomew's Hospital. Hogarth's eventual capture of this commission, which was to go in a public place in the City, led Vertue to describe him as having 'a good Front' and being 'a Scheemist', for he achieved it by what Vertue called sarcastically the 'noble artifice' of giving the paintings free of charge, by courting the Hospital Governors whose ranks he joined as a result of his charitable act.

Hogarth had to employ guile to get the commission, but he was also motivated by a genuine desire to promote the interests of native artists, by reaffirming that a painter without Italian experience could make a creditable attempt at the genre. Vertue's verdict was that 'it is by every one judged to be more than coud be expected of him', and there is an element of hubris in Hogarth's attempt at the Great Style without a proper academic training or the experience of an apprenticeship to a practitioner of the genre. The problems of such painting were not just technical, of making a convincing illusion on a large scale: they also required an approach to the theoretical question of the depiction of the realm of ideal moral action. The subjects chosen, in keeping with their setting in a hospital, were the Pool of Bethesda and the Good Samaritan, and it was inevitable that Hogarth should seek authority for his design in earlier masters. The chief influence on the *Bethesda* painting is the Raphael of the great Cartoons, filtered through the

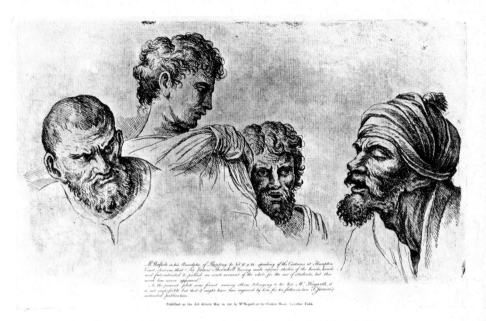

72 *Heads from the Raphael Cartoons*, engraving by Hogarth, after Thornhill?

classical style adopted by Thornhill for his grisaille paintings in the cupola   *13*
of St Paul's Cathedral.

Such parentage is surprising if we think of Hogarth as he often portrayed
himself, as a chauvinistic Englishman who had nothing but contempt for
the Old Masters. In later life he claimed that he would rather be the author
of *The Stages of Cruelty* than of the Raphael Cartoons. However, he   *141, 142*
qualified this by claiming to 'speak as a man not as an artist', and he made it
clear that his objections were not to Raphael so much as to the thoughtless
imitation of earlier artists. In the early 1730s Hogarth must have been
steeped in the Raphael Cartoons, for Thornhill was working on his copies
when Hogarth was lodging with him, and there is evidence that Hogarth
was preparing a set of engravings after those copies. In the early eighteenth   *72*
century Raphael was as much admired for precision of physiognomy and
expression as for his grasp of elevated form, and Thornhill was planning to
publish from the Cartoons, as Vertue tells us, 'a book of the heads hands &
feet & other parts of those most excellent designs for the use of students in
the Art of Painting & Sculpture' – a drawing book, like those of Le Brun
and others, in which the heads and gestures are analysed as models of
expression.

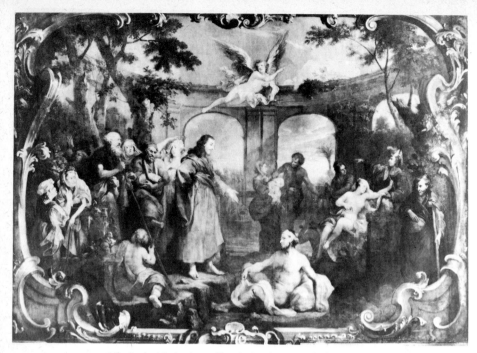

73 *The Pool of Bethesda*, wall-painting in St Bartholomew's Hospital, London, 1735–37

73   This fragmented approach is undoubtedly reflected in *The Pool of Bethesda*, and it is possible to see the painting on one level as a product of Hogarth's incomplete understanding of the Great Style. The naked sick man in the foreground and the rich lady to the right are based on careful 74 academic studies of the nude and contribute to the ideal nature of the painting: the figures of the sick on the left are, on the other hand, so medically convincing and vigorous in their grotesquery that they bring us back to the world of satire. The setting with the curved arcade behind is Raphael-via-Thornhill, while the framing festoons with the dog leaning over into our space are derived from late Baroque wall-decoration. The figure of Christ is wholly disastrous and quite shapeless. A reminder of the painter of modern subjects is to be found in the invented incident on the right, of the rich lady being carried to the pool by servants, one of whom pushes a poor woman with her child out of the way in order that his mistress should be first in the water after the angel had stirred it up (John 5:2).

    Hogarth invokes the divine and the charitable aspects of healing, and in 75 the companion painting of *The Good Samaritan* practical charity is celebrated. It is contrasted first with religion based on authority, symbolized

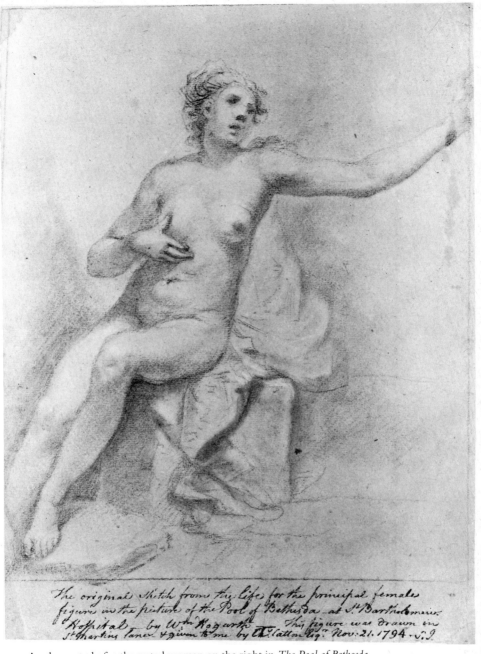

The original Sketch from the Life for the principal female
figures in the picture of the Pool of Bethesda at St Bartholomew
Hospital by Wm. Hogarth This figure was drawn in
St Martins Lane & given to me by Th: Fallon Esqr Nov. 21. 1794. J.I

74   Academy study for the seated woman on the right in *The Pool of Bethesda*

by a Levite in the background demanding obeisance from a prostrate figure, and secondly with religion based on textual authority, represented by a priestly figure absorbed in a book, both of whom pass by on the other side. Hogarth must surely have received advice on these subjects from Bishop Hoadly, who had preached a sermon on the subject and with whose views on the supremacy of works over faith the paintings were in entire conformity. The paintings also represent Hogarth's first contact with charitable institutions, and there is every evidence that he took his duties as Governor seriously. He was disappointed, however, at least for the time being, in the failure of the work to bring in more commissions. The paintings, as far as we know, attracted nothing but admiration – indeed they became one of the sights of the town – but the Burlington party would not have helped him to repeat his success. Furthermore the ascendency of Palladian taste had tended to reduce the demand for illusionistic Baroque wall-paintings of the Thornhill type in favour of severely compartmentalized ceilings and walls, which were more likely than ever to contain the work of imported masters.

The hegemony of the Palladians and the refusal of patrons to see the English school emerging beneath their noses led Hogarth to counter-attack. In a letter published in a newspaper on 7 June 1737 Hogarth, under the patriotic name 'Britophil', defended Thornhill's achievement at Greenwich, and attacked the taste, encouraged by middlemen, for 'dead Christs, holy families Madonas, and other dismal dark objects'.

Irresistible though Hogarth's claims may seem to be in retrospect, the career of Kent advanced regardless: he became Architect and Master Carpenter to the King in 1737, thus cutting Hogarth off forever from royal patronage. The French portrait-painter J. B. Vanloo (1684–1745) came over in 1737 and had an immediate fashionable success, which Hogarth's challenge with *Captain Coram* (see Chapter 7) did little to abate, and a new 'genius', Giles Hussey (1710–88), became the darling of the fashionable, though Vertue tells us that he 'Idles his time in the Country with a relation, sketches a little, begins, but makes no conclusion, talks of mighty things'. Vertue's summing up of the year 1738 concludes that the art of painting is 'neither getting nor looseing', and his list of those artists 'who draw and Colour masterly' does not mention Hogarth. Aristocratic taste and the fashion for the new and exotic were refusing to give way before Hogarth's seemingly unanswerable logic.

96
101

102

75   Detail of *The Good Samaritan*, wall-painting in St Bartholomew's Hospital, London, 1735–37

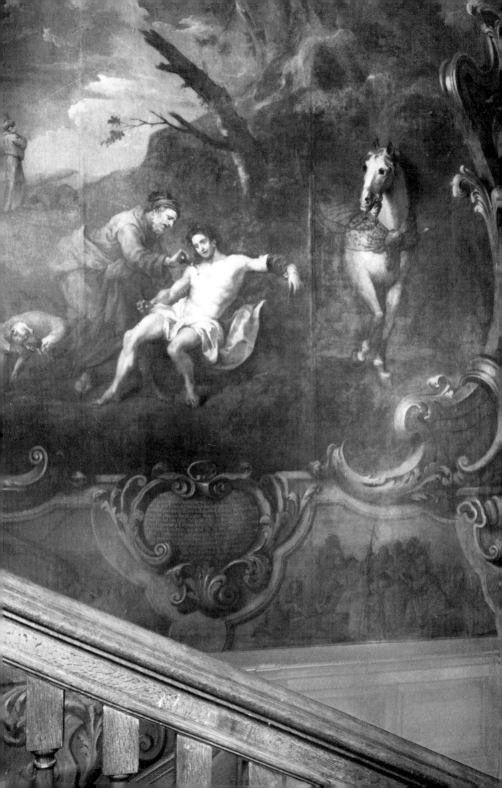

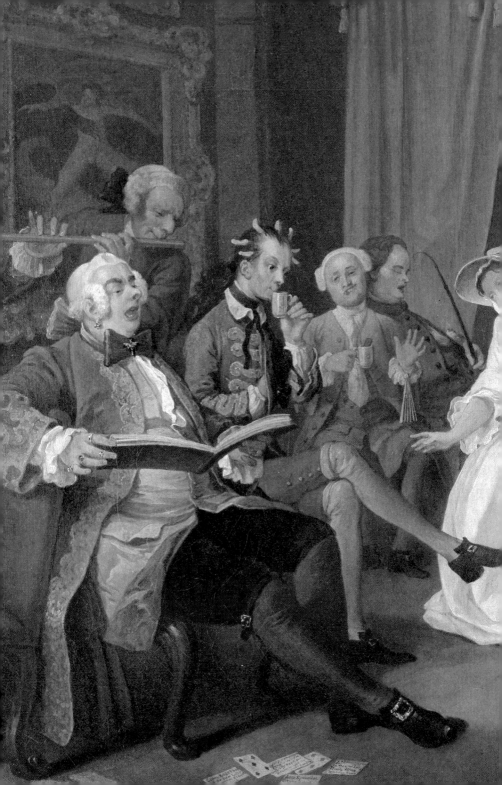

CHAPTER SIX

The Connoisseurs and Comic History Painting

THE 1730S WERE FOR HOGARTH a decade of continual experimentation in new genres and extension of those already attempted. The 1740s by that token were years of consolidation in which he sought to bring theory and practice together and thus win over the nation to the idea of an English school of art. In pursuit of this objective Hogarth had by the end of the 1740s painted an exemplary body of work and offered new possibilities in the publishing of engravings, the teaching of art, and the exhibition of paintings. Many of these initiatives were commenced in the 1730s, but it is in the 1740s that the 'respectable' Hogarth emerges with an art of definable social function and theoretical substructure.

In the early 1730s Hogarth had cultivated a certain notoriety for himself through the press and society, and by reading Vertue's annals we can chart the transformation of the 'scheemist' of the 1730s to the hypersensitive personality who emerges in the mid-1740s, when he had failed to alter the views of the connoisseurs. Yet Hogarth was never without influential supporters, among them men equally creative in their own fields, like Henry Fielding and David Garrick. The keynote of the new decade is established for Hogarth in Fielding's article on satire in *The Champion* of 10 June 1740, which commends the artist as 'one of the most useful Satyrists any Age hath produced'. Fielding claimed that the Progresses were 'calculated more to serve the Cause of Virtue, and for the preservation of Mankind, than all the Folios of Morality which have ever been written'.

Apart from a personal acquaintanceship going back to the early 1730s, Hogarth would have known Fielding (1707–54) mainly as a comic playwright. In 1740 he was about to establish himself as a serious novelist, but up to then his reputation was that of a lightweight, a man about town, author of farces and Grub Street polemics. Hogarth's role in Fielding's career was, in a nutshell, to provide him with the example of a body of work which was both humorous and deeply serious, and improving without being sententious. In return Fielding played a major part in helping Hogarth to construct a theoretical framework for his notions of satire. In the years 1742 and 1743 we can observe a kind of theoretical dialogue between writer and painter carried on from work to work. Fielding's famous preface to *Joseph Andrews* (1742), in which Hogarth is commended in the highest terms, is answered

105

76   Musicians and dancing master at the Countess's Levée: detail of scene 4 of *Marriage-a-la-Mode*, 1743 (see ill. 82)

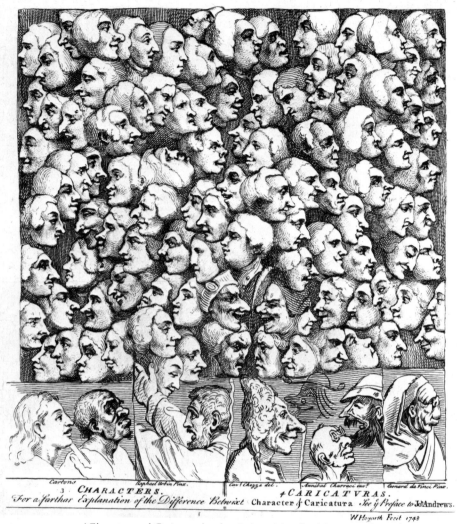

Cartons   Raphael Urbin Pinx.   Cav.l Chezze del.   Annibal Charraci inv.t   Leonard da Vinci Pinx.
3   CHARACTERS.   4 CARICATVRAS.
For a farthar Explanation of the Difference Betwixt Character & Caricatura See ÿ Preface to Jo:Andrews.

W Hogarth Fecit 1743

77   'Characters and Caricaturas', subscription ticket for Marriage-a-la-Mode, engraving, second state, 1743

by Hogarth's direction on the subscription ticket for *Marriage-a-la-Mode*
(1743): 'For a farthar Explanation of the Difference Betwixt Character &
Caricatura See ye Preface to Joh. Andrews.' Fielding's preface attributes to
Hogarth the creation of an art form which is elevating and yet truthful
about human nature. He gave the artist a definition of a middle way
between History painting, in which the pictorial drama is enacted at a
deliberate distance from the world of experience, and the 'low' genre of
caricature, which consists of the distortion of a fragment of reality for
comic effect. This middle way implies the depiction not of gods or grotesques but what Hogarth calls 'character', and a process which Fielding
describes as expressing 'the Affections of Men on Canvas'. 'Caricature' is for
Hogarth what 'burlesque' is for Fielding, a farcical distortion which reduces
men to one salient physical characteristic – 'a Nose, or any other Feature
of a preposterous size, or . . . in some absurd or monstrous Attitude'.
'Character', on the other hand, can show the whole man as a thinking and
feeling being. Fielding said of Hogarth, 'It hath been thought a vast
Commendation of a Painter, to say his Figures seem to breathe; but surely,
it is a much greater and nobler Applause, that they appear to think.'

Fielding calls Hogarth a 'Comic History-Painter', and this paradoxical
formulation precisely parallels his own description of *Joseph Andrews* as a
'comic epic in prose'. By learned reference to classical precedent, Fielding
thus elevated the comic to the moral level of the tragic, and in so doing he
provided Hogarth with a clear answer to the connoisseurs who regarded his
art as less serious than the Old Masters. For Hogarth it was the last theoretical
nail in the coffin of those who used classical arguments to thwart the
development of a native school. This unexpected praise for his Modern
Moral Subjects undoubtedly led him to contemplate another series in the
genre now dignified by the name of Comic History Painting, but unfortunately for him, the logic of his position failed to destroy the doubters'
complacency. Indeed, the more Hogarth built up his theoretical structure
the more vulnerable he became to his own weapon: ridicule.

Why did Hogarth encounter such a resistance to his ideas? There were, in
fact, within the discussion of the time perfectly reasonable objections to his
claims. Hogarth's parodies of connoisseurs and their taste for darkened Old
Masters are so amusing that one forgets that they are a complete travesty.
There were, no doubt, dealers who sold to ignorant aristocrats expensive
paintings in 'Alesso Baldovenetto's second and best manner', but the true
connoisseurs like Richardson and Reynolds rested their case on an experience of the great works of Raphael and Michelangelo; they sought to
educate patrons towards a higher understanding of the greatest art in order
to set high standards for English artists. Hogarth, of course, yielded to no

one in his admiration for the great Renaissance masters, but his habit of satire was too strong for him to be fair to those who felt that the Old Masters could be successfully emulated. His own appraisals of the great masters of the past were too irreverent for the taste of most of his contemporaries, and he knew very well that people chose to misunderstand him. His provocative manner of conversation about other painters is caught by Vertue, who must often have heard him sound off in company: under the year 1745 Vertue notes:

[Hogarth] dispised under-valud all other present, & preceedent painters, such as Kneller Lilly Vandyke – those English painters, of the highest Reputation – such reasonings or envious detractions he not only often or at all times – made the subject of his conversations & Observations to Gentlemen and Lovers of Art But such like invidiuous reflections he would argue & maintain with all sorts of Artists painters sculptors etc.

Hogarth himself admitted half-defiantly that he might have gone too far:

by this Idle way of proceeding [i.e. using his method of direct observation] I grew so profane as to admire Nature beyond Pictures and I confess sometimes objected to the devinity of even Raphael Urbin Corregio and Michael Angelo for which I have been severly treated.

79–85   Hogarth does not in fact call the *Marriage-a-la-Mode* paintings, which he began in 1743, Comic History, but his newspaper advertisement for them makes it plain that he considered them to be on a more dignified level than his two Progresses. The theme was concerned with 'a Variety of Modern Occurrences in High Life', and particular care was now to be taken to avoid objection to 'the Decency or Elegancy of the whole work'. By claiming that 'none of the Characters represented shall be personal', he explicitly repudiated the references to well-known contemporaries which had contributed to the notoriety of the previous cycles, and made a claim to the universality which was the *sine qua non* of History painting. We are warned against seeking prototypes for the protagonists in the *Marriage-a-la-Mode*, but equally we are expected to see them as thinking beings, not abstract types.

Despite the closeness of his ideas to those of Fielding's novels, Hogarth had in mind the conventions not of a novel but of a play, and in his *Autobiographical Notes* he continually seeks an analogy in the stage: 'let figure[s] be consider[ed] as Actors dresed for the sublime genteel comedy or same in high or low life'. Here his friendship with David Garrick (1717–79) is material. In 1741 the actor had made his sensational debut as Richard III, a role in which he was to be painted by Hogarth in 1745. Garrick's distinction

108

was to ensure the triumph of a more naturalistic style of acting: in Paulson's words, he 'transformed Richard III from the bloodthirsty stock villain of the old productions into a complex tragic character'. He gave his characters the complexity of real men by a restrained and natural use of physiognomy and gesture, which he learned from observation of life and also from paintings. Garrick was as successful in comic as in tragic roles, and behind this versatility lay the recognition that Shakespeare did not make a rigid distinction between genres; humour could enter into tragedy, and comedy could be profound and instructive. The commonly held notion that despite his great virtues Shakespeare's disregard of the classical rules made his work essentially defective was in the 1740s giving way to the belief expressed by William Warburton, that he was an author who 'let us into the knowledge of our nature'. Warburton commends Shakespeare also for 'the amazing sagacity with which he investigates every hidden spring and wheel of human Action; or his happy manner of communicating this knowledge, in the just and living paintings which he has given us of all our Passions, Appetites and Pursuits'. There are numerous indications of Hogarth's love of Shakespeare, the definitive expression being the *Self-Portrait* of 1745, where his own portrait, and by implication his art, rests 119 upon the foundation of volumes of Shakespeare, Milton and Swift.

It seems odd, given Hogarth's claims for English art, that the *Marriage-a-la-Mode* series should have required French engravers. But while he disdained the painstaking pursuit of elegance associated with the French manner practiced by Gravelot, Baron and other engravers who moved between England and France, he was genuinely modest about his own technical accomplishments, claiming that he was too lazy to excel in fine work. As the series was to deal with the 'High Life' it was essential that the engraving should be in an elegant manner, for the very elegance of the final result contains an element of satire. Hogarth went to Paris in May 1743, when the paintings for the *Marriage* were probably largely completed, to procure engravers, and Vertue also tells us that he went 'to cultivate knowledge or improve his Stock of Ass[urance]'. There is a strong hint of Rococo feeling in the *Marriage* paintings, but it does not necessarily prove the direct influence of what he saw in Paris: he knew Gravelot and Hayman well enough to be aware of the French style. He would have been familiar with paintings of the type of *Le Lecteur* (Marble Hill House, Twickenham) by 78 Gravelot, in which the polite world is depicted with grace and elegance. This French naturalism, also to be found in Hayman's paintings, has little in common with seventeenth-century Dutch realism, but exhibits a certain casualness and friendly intimacy within an aura of discreet wealth and social position.

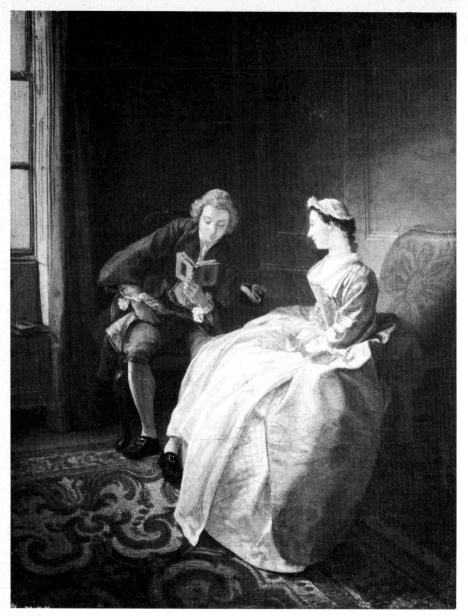

78   Hubert Gravelot: *Le Lecteur*, or *The Judicious Lover*

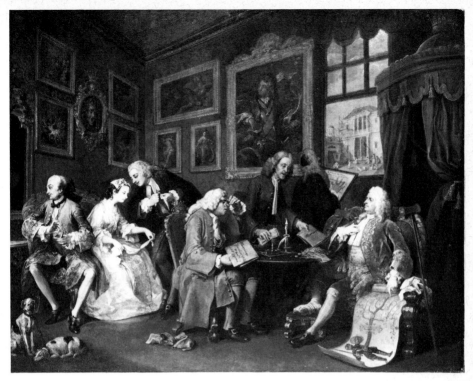

79 *Marriage-a-la-Mode*, I: the Marriage Contract, 1743

The perceived difference between Dutch and French naturalism counter-
points the drama of the *Marriage* series. Hogarth associates the French style
with the gay amoral life of the great houses of the West End. In the first
painting the Earl, despite his gouty condition, reclines in an affectation of   *79*
Watteauesque grace, while the merchant has the squat inelegant form of a
Dutch burgher. The heir, on the left, is a Frenchified fop oblivious to
feeling, while his future wife reveals by signs of emotion her lower social
class. A large portrait on the Earl's wall depicts him in a telling parody of a
French court portrait of the Louis XIV type, posing with ridiculous non-
chalance on the battlefield, whereas the merchant is shown at the end of the
series as owning a houseful of the most vulgar and boorish Dutch paintings.   *84*
If the dress and attitudes of the aristocracy are French their art and architecture are mainly Italian; needless to say they have a complete disregard for
native talent. In the Countess's Morning Levée virtually all those providing
services (with the exception of the lawyer Silvertongue) are demonstrably   *76, 82*

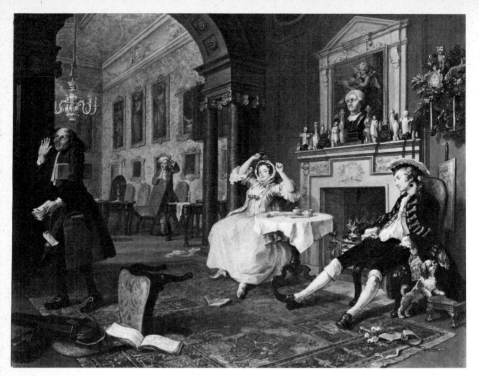

80, 81   *Marriage-a-la-Mode*, II: After the Marriage, 1743

foreign. There is throughout the six designs an insistent connection between
the taste for foreign art and affectation and immorality.

Works of art are omnipresent in the *Marriage-a-la-Mode*; they serve as
catalyst to the action and comment on it. The need for the Earl to sell his son
in marriage comes from his fashionable extravagance in building a vast
Palladian mansion with a pretentious double loggia which can be seen in
the first picture. The paintings on the Earl's wall represent the taste of
connoisseurs for darkened Old Masters, and the subjects of martyrdoms
and assaults on the human body refer also to the depredations of the Earl's
creditors. The possibilities for humour are infinite; a wall-mirror with a
sconce has, instead of a reflecting glass, a hideous gorgon's head, and the
ceiling painting of Pharaoh being drowned in the Red Sea suggests a
ludicrous breach of decorum in placing a watery scene at a great height, a
80, 81   joke at the expense of the wall-painters. The scene After the Marriage
26   contains reminders of the kind of conversation piece, like *The Wollaston*

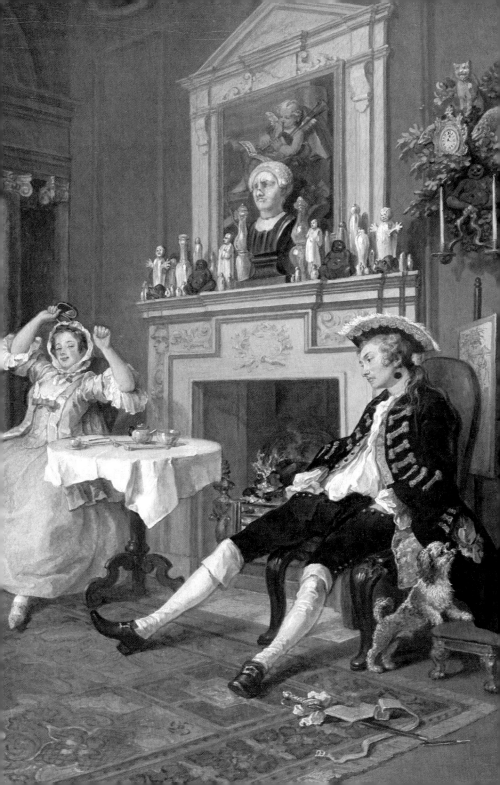

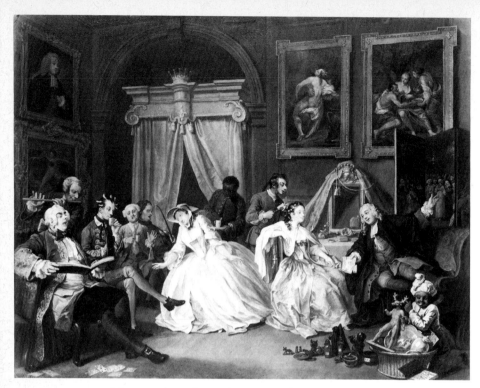

82　*Marriage-a-la-Mode*, IV: the Countess's Levée, 1743 (see also ill. 76)

Family, which Hogarth had so often painted in the previous decade. Elegant dress and card playing are seen as part of a world of aimless pleasure-seeking and extravagance, and the miserable expression on the heir's face suggests that boredom and regret follow on the heels of empty pleasure. On the other hand the steward who comments despairingly on a sheaf of bills is treated with no more sympathy; a book entitled *Regeneration* sticking out of his pocket reveals him to be an 'Enthusiast' and follower of a chillingly Puritanical sect. The unpaid bills and the Kentian interior suggests the son is following in his father's footsteps, and he has carried bad taste to even more inventive heights by purchasing such creations as the elaborate clock-cum-wall sconce and Chinese porcelain. Hogarth's criticism of the heir's taste is, in its own way, perfectly conventional. He objects above all to breaches of decorum or propriety, for example in placing an erotic picture of a Jovian *amour* on the same wall as a group of saints, or surrounding a fake Roman bust with Chinese objects, in themselves examples of irregular taste.

114

In the elaborate room settings in *Marriage-a-la-Mode* a fatal impropriety undermines even the consistency of the false taste. In the Countess's Levée 〔82〕 the erotic paintings of *Jupiter and Io* by Correggio and *Lot and his Daughters*, which preside over her dalliance with Silvertongue, are balanced by *The Rape of Ganymede*, which refers covertly to the sexual proclivities of the 〔76〕 epicene foreigners beneath. But even the consistency of the erotic theme is broken by a bland and austere clerical portrait.

The elaborate settings should not detract, however, from the human tragedy which stems from the marriage of convenience. Hogarth creates an undercurrent of real emotion and feeling which transcends the comedy of manners. The possibility of affection between the young couple is destroyed by the false positions in which they have been placed by their parents, for they are forced out of a natural relationship based on love, into conventional roles as rake and woman of pleasure. This sense of what might have been elevates the series to tragedy. As the young Earl dies from a wound inflicted by Silvertongue in the bagnio, the Countess does not follow her lover out 〔83, 85〕 of the window, but kneels before her husband aghast at what she has lost. We move from the Countess's Levée, the world of masquerade and illicit affairs, to a scene of darkness and tragedy. Her own death in the final paint- 〔84〕 ing takes place not in the ephemeral world of fashion but in the home of her miserly father, who is intent only upon removing her ring.

These hints of moral and emotional complexity make the *Marriage-a-la-Mode* series as much superior to the twelve illustrations for Richardson's *Pamela* by Joseph Highmore (1692–1780) as Fielding's *Joseph Andrews* is to 〔86〕 the earlier novel. Even so it would be wrong to make too close a comparison between Hogarth's work of the 1740s and Fielding's two great novels of the same decade. Good deeds and unexpected kindnesses do occur in Hogarth's moral series, but their appearance hardly counteracts the domination of immorality and foolishness in his world. *Joseph Andrews* and *Tom Jones* (1749) both contain fully rounded characters like Parson Adams, who have their weaknesses but who are entirely on the side of virtue. Hogarth's stance as a satirist was governed by the notion that it was enough to reveal the follies and vices of mankind. Yet he could hardly have been oblivious to the shift among novelists like Richardson and Fielding towards a greater concern with benevolence – a desire not just to castigate vice, but to show that virtue could eventually triumph.

Perhaps in response to this change of mood Hogarth began to work on a sequel to *Marriage-a-la-Mode*, entitled *The Happy Marriage*, which survives only in a number of oil sketches and engravings after lost paintings. *The* 〔127, 128〕 *Happy Marriage* may have been, as Paulson suggests, a direct response to the success of Highmore's *Pamela* illustrations, but Hogarth's abortive series as

115

(*overleaf*)
83, 85 *Marriage-a-la-Mode*, V: the Death of the Earl, 1743
84 *Marriage-a-la-Mode*, VI: the Death of the Countess, 1743

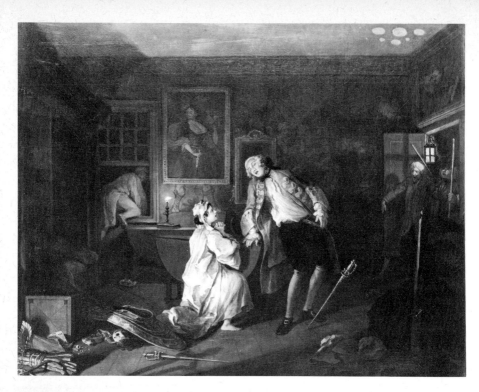

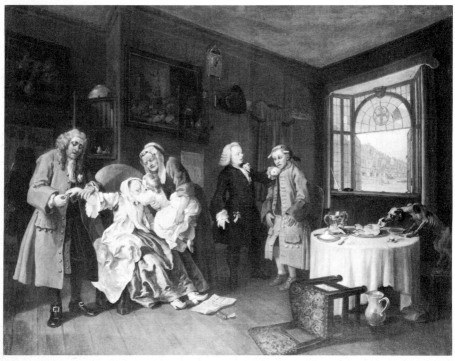

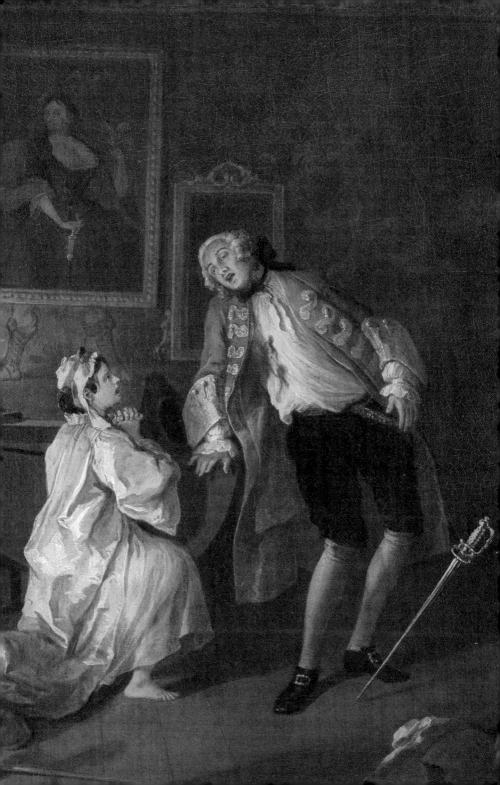

it survives seems to be quite without plot. The known oil sketches depict episodes in a country wedding, which appears to encounter no obstacle, or to sustain any drama. Hogarth was obviously not satisfied with them, and his failure to finish them drew the sarcasm of John Wilkes (as will be discussed in the last chapter). In fact they contain some of Hogarth's most beautiful painting, and they foreshadow a desire to provide a path of virtue, as well as an anatomy of vice, which reached fruition in the *Industry and Idleness* series of 1747.

Hogarth continued to paint large-scale Biblical works when the opportunity arose, and they show signs of increased grasp and consolidation. *Paul*

87 *before Felix* in Lincoln's Inn makes his earlier paintings for St Bartholomew's

73, 75 Hospital seem pathetically ill-formed. It is distinguished by a new clarity of approach in which Hogarth's notion of character is applied to an elevated subject. The choice of subject and scale invite direct comparison with the

13 Raphael Cartoons and with Thornhill's Pauline cycle in St Paul's. The

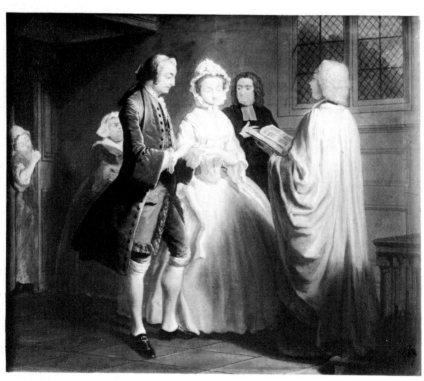

86   Joseph Highmore: *Pamela is Married*, 1743–44

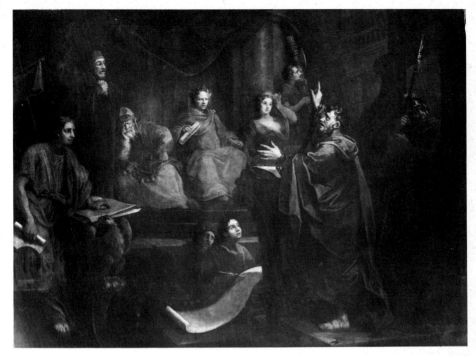

87 *Paul before Felix*, 1748

solemnity of the moment, in which Paul proclaims to the Roman Governor
Felix the transcendence of Divine over temporal justice, even that of the
Roman Empire, was appropriate to the intended setting, in the Chapel of
Lincoln's Inn. Hogarth has avoided the high-minded blandness of Thornhill's painting by stressing the individual physiognomy of each figure, and
he has chosen to emphasize St Paul's prophetic fire rather than the classical
nobility of the Raphael prototype, using vast enfolding drapes to bring
out the grandeur of the Apostle's figure. The Roman Governor's earth-
bound justice is revealed in his expression and the figure of his wife Drusilla,
who appears as a bored and uncomprehending courtesan.

The other major History painting of this period, *Moses brought to* 88, 89
Pharaoh's Daughter, painted in 1746 for the Foundling Hospital, is notable
for its warmth of feeling, far surpassing in tenderness and humour the other
three paintings in the same room by Hayman, Highmore and Wills. By
contrast Hayman's *Finding of Moses* is a static and academic version of 90
Poussin, without the intellectual rigour of that master.

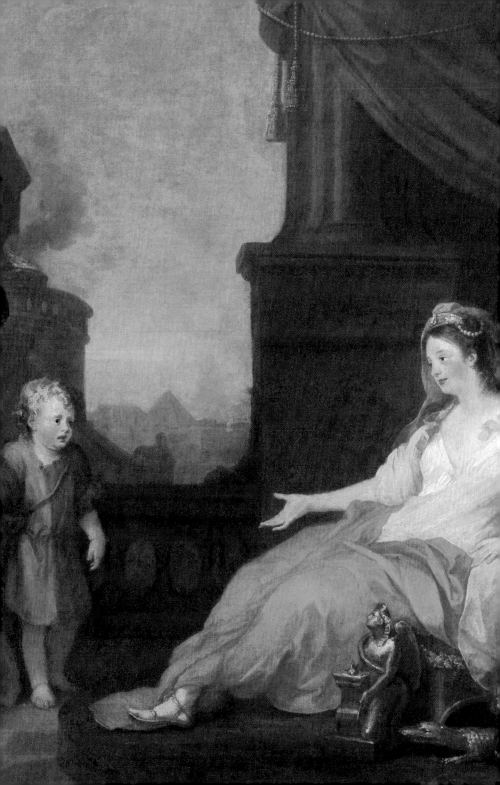

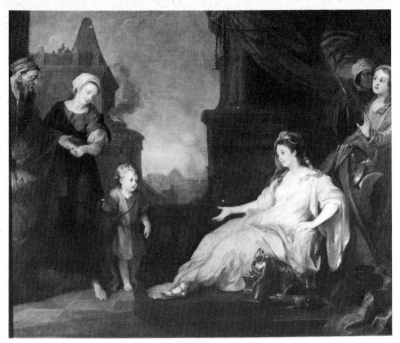

88, 89 *Moses brought to Pharaoh's Daughter*, 1746

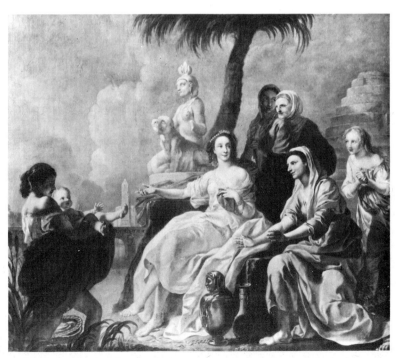

90 Francis Hayman: *The Finding of Moses*, 1746

Something of Hogarth's desire to humanize traditional genres of painting can be glimpsed in one of his few recorded attempts at a classical subject. We have a tantalizingly brief account by Horace Walpole of a lost painting of *Danaë*, in which he tells us that 'Danae herself is a meer nymph of Drury' and that 'the old nurse tries a coin of the golden shower with her teeth, to see if it is true gold'. Now this picture might have been a parody of the erotic paintings of Titian or Correggio, as Paulson has suggested, but it could also have been a demonstration that naturalism is not necessarily incompatible with mythology: Danaë's desire and the nurse's reaction could be human as well as divine.

Hogarth's experiments with naturalism exposed him to the accusation that by bringing realism into the elevated style he was merely diminishing it. The Dutch painters of the seventeenth century were universally thought in Hogarth's time to lack any conception of the ideal, and to be incapable of producing any art not based on direct observation. Hogarth showed an outward agreement with this point of view in the taste of the merchant in 84 *Marriage-a-la-Mode* for tavern scenes and pictures of pissing boors, and in 92 the subscription ticket to the engravings of *Paul before Felix* and *Moses brought to Pharaoh's Daughter* he provided a burlesque of *Paul before Felix* 'in

91 Drawing, possibly for a lost painting of *Danaë*

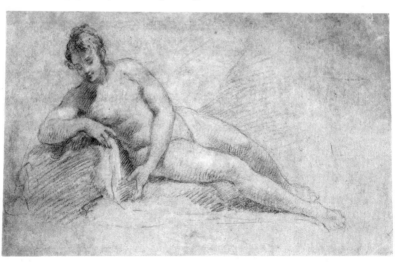

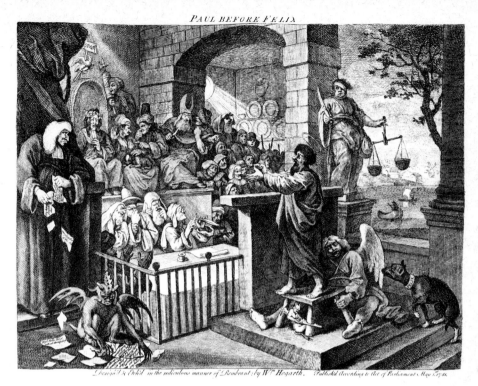

92   Burlesque of *Paul before Felix* (ill. 87), engraving, 1751

the rediculous manner of Rembrant'. It shows, with grotesque exaggeration, how the subject of Hogarth's picture would have been treated if a
Dutch master had painted it. It is a compendium of visual jokes all pertain-
ing to the same idea, which is the tendency of Dutch artists to reduce every
serious idea to everyday banality. One is intended to compare the natural
grandeur and power of Paul in Hogarth's painting with the tiny little figure   *87, 92*
of the Apostle in the burlesque, who needs to stand on a stool to be seen over
the witness box. The stool itself is held by a fat angel who has dropped off
to sleep while an imp saws through its leg. The audience is made up of
ignorant boors, and there is a deliberately gratuitous background of plate
on a dresser and a view of Holland outside. The ticket is a good illustration
of the differences between high and low art; but the danger was that people
would draw the wrong conclusion and assume that an artist who could
burlesque his own compositions was incapable of really aspiring to the true
elevation of the Raphael Cartoons – a point, it must be admitted, that is not
without substance.

123

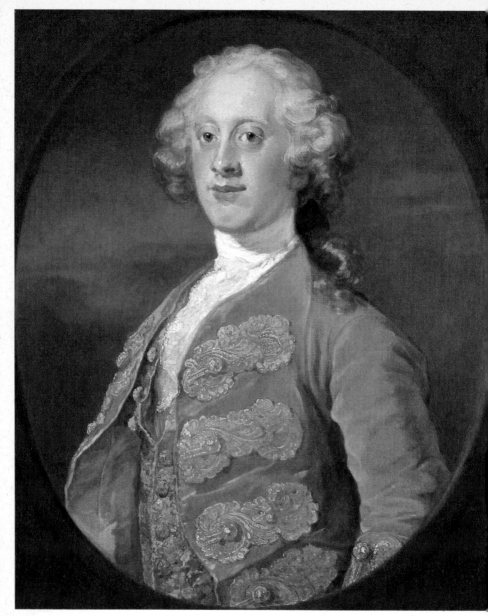

93   *William Cavendish, 4th Duke of Devonshire*, 1741

CHAPTER SEVEN

Portrait Painting

HOGARTH MADE PORTRAITS in most periods of his life, and at certain times, in the early 1740s and at the end of his life, he attempted to establish a regular practice. Nonetheless he was never a professional 'face painter' in the conventional eighteenth-century sense. Almost every commission was consciously approached as a unique venture, and he deliberately avoided the practice of making portrait painting 'a kind of manufacture', in which the procedure was standardized to allow for the division of labour and the production of replicas. He did not take on pupils or apprentices, and he remained deliberately aloof from the studio practice of the great succession of fashionable portrait painters from Van Dyck through Lely and Kneller to Jonathan Richardson and Thomas Hudson (1701–79) in his own time. For the most part Hogarth's paintings are of personal friends or men of similar background, who were content not to aspire to senatorial dignity but to be depicted with freshness and realism. He sought to capture the 'speaking likeness': the head caught at the moment of maximum vivacity, engaged in animated conversation revealing the sitter's most characteristic wisdom.

If we compare the portraits of the 4th Duke of Devonshire by Hogarth 93 (Yale Center for British Art) and by Thomas Hudson (National Trust, 94 Hardwick Hall), even if the latter is probably only a copy, we find the Hogarth to be in conception more sprightly and *mouvementé*; the head and body are given equal expressive vitality by the broad vigorous brushwork which emphasizes the plasticity and relief of the forms. On close inspection we can see that Hogarth has applied his brush especially freely to the moving parts of the face, the eyelids, mouth and nostrils, so that they are less defined, yet they also appear to protrude beyond the plane of the face, giving it an almost humorous assertiveness. By contrast in the Hudson these parts of the face are circumscribed by its overall shape, and the effect is of grave formality.

The same artists also portrayed Archbishop Herring, following the 95 familiar type of ecclesiastical portrait which goes back to Raphael's *Julius II*. Hogarth's (Tate Gallery) manages to be both superciliously grand and extremely vivacious: a prince of the Church who would be at home at the court of Louis XIV, but on this evidence a man of rich humanity and wit. Hudson's portrait (Corpus Christi College, Cambridge) made Herring

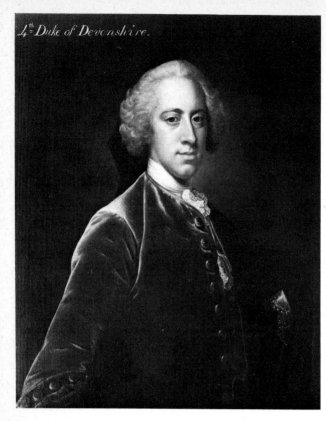

4ᵗʰ Duke of Devonshire.

94 After Thomas Hudson:
*William Cavendish, 4th Duke
of Devonshire*

look stodgy and dull, a churchman of comfortable thoughts and regular dinners; the gestures are hesitant, the face without animation. Yet it appears that the Archbishop and his friends disliked Hogarth's painting intensely, and Hudson seems to have been called in to provide a more acceptable image of which replicas would be made. Such a preference might seem extraordinary; nevertheless, only a minority of patrons wanted to be painted with Hogarthian directness, not so much because his portraits were thought to be unflattering but because their assertiveness offended the prevailing sense of decorum.

Hudson's success was based on the ability to catch a likeness, a graceful use of draperies, which were well known to have been usually the work of his drapery painter Joseph van Aken, and, as Vertue put it, 'a manner agreable without affected manner of painting'. Unfortunately for Hudson, and others who practised the middle way in portraiture at the end of the 1730s, these were precisely the qualities in which the French excelled, so it is not surprising that English artists should have been so put out of joint by

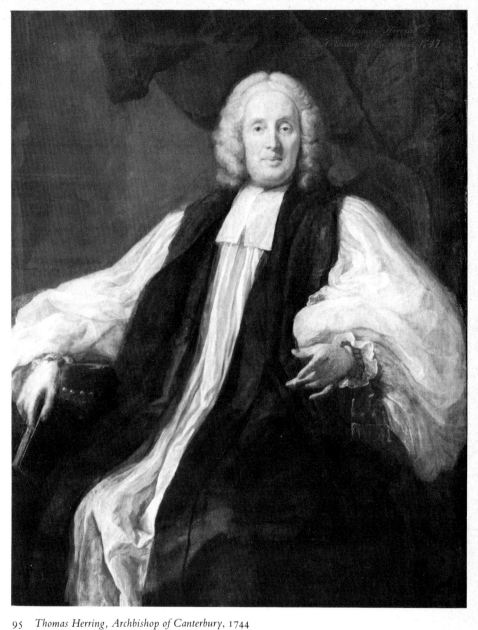

95   *Thomas Herring, Archbishop of Canterbury*, 1744

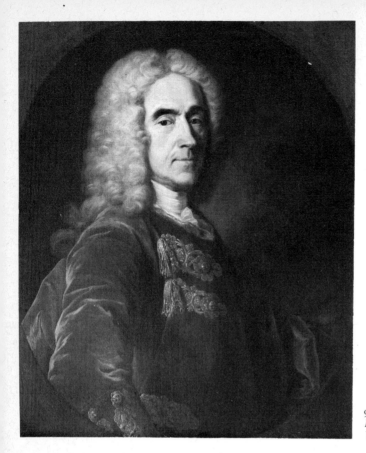

96   J. B. Vanloo:
*Richard Temple, 1st
Viscount Cobham*

the arrival of the French painter J. B. Vanloo late in 1737. According to Vertue, 'the great employment in six months from his first comeing exceeds any other painter that is come to England in the memory of any one living . . . but the English painters have had great uneasiness [that] it has much blemished their reputation – and business'. Certainly Vanloo's

96   portraits are drawn with more precision and individuality than those of Hudson, and they have a certain dash and playfulness, but one can sympathize with the dismay felt by Hogarth – momentarily siding with his rivals against the foreign invader – at the ease with which the fashionable and wealthy followed the new star.

Hogarth's early single-figure portraits employ essentially the same conventions as the conversation pieces of the early 1730s. What is probably

97   the earliest, the small portrait of 1730 of Sir Robert Pye (Marble Hill House, Twickenham) shows Sir Robert seated languidly in a vaguely

128

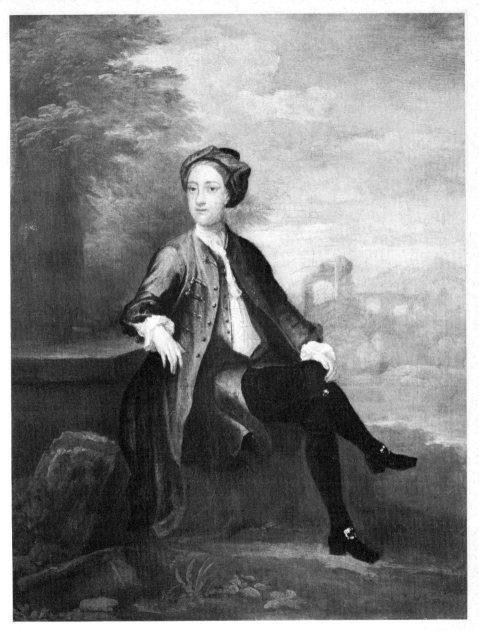

97   *Sir Robert Pye*, 1730

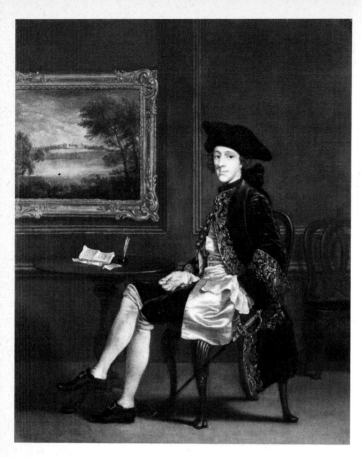

36   classical landscape. The feeling, like that in *The Ashley Cowper Family*, is
     predominantly French. Landscape and background continued to play an
     important part in his small portraits of the 1730s, as they did in the work of
98   Francis Hayman and the more provincial artists of the next generation like
     Arthur Devis (1711–87) and the young Thomas Gainsborough (1727–88).
     It may be that the friendly and unpompous atmosphere of this type of
     painting was more suited to country gentry than metropolitan grandees.
        Hogarth's interest in a grander and more ambitious type of portrait
     began to grow in the late 1730s, perhaps stimulated by his experiments with
     History painting, as well as by a desire to present himself as the leader
     and spokesman of his profession. The transition from his early manner to
     the more dignified style of the 1740s can best be observed by comparing
99   his two seated portraits of his friend Bishop Hoadly, one of *c.* 1738 (Hunting-

     130

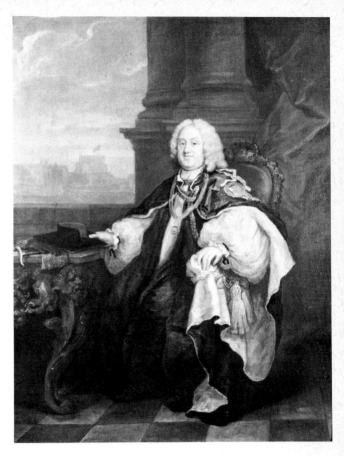

ton Library, San Marino) and a much larger one of *c.* 1743 (Tate Gallery).   *100*
The paintings are similar in their use of the robes and trappings of high
ecclesiastical office, but in the earlier portrait Hoadly appears small and
dwarfed by these accoutrements, whereas in the later work he fills the
picture commandingly, his robes now a natural adornment of his
magnificence.

Hogarth's first major success in his new manner was the great seated
figure of the philanthropist Captain Coram, which he painted in 1740 for   *101*
the Foundling Hospital in London, of which he had become a Governor in
1739. Hogarth tells us that he deliberately attempted a 'mighty portrait'
which would serve as a spirited riposte to Vanloo, in order to rally the
British portrait painters to regain their lost clientele. Hogarth's own account
of his motives, however, does little justice to the richness and complexity

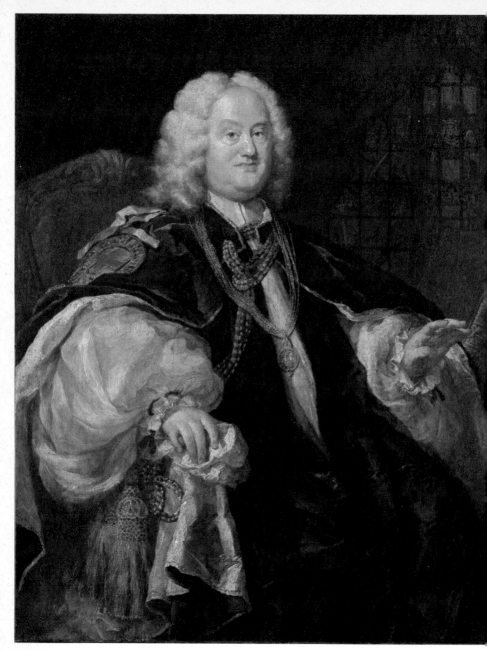

100   *Benjamin Hoadly, Bishop of Winchester, c.* 1743 (Tate version)

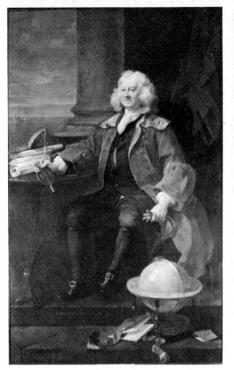
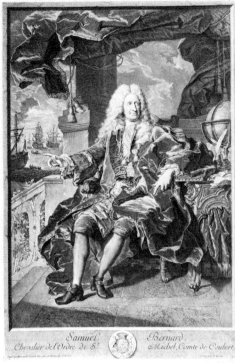

101   *Captain Thomas Coram*, 1740 (see also ill. 133)

102   (*right*) After Hyacinthe Rigaud: *Samuel Bernard*, engraving by Pierre Drevet,
1729 (compare ills. 101 and 106)

of reference in this great picture. One might argue that the robustness of the
physiognomy reveals a certain Englishness, but the painting is as much
French as English in spirit, and the imperious grandeur of the setting and the
sitter's drapery recall the state portraits of Louis XIV's court. The primary
source for the composition is certainly the engraving after Hyacinthe
Rigaud's grand portrait of Samuel Bernard of 1729: if the borrowing were   102
conscious it would make clear Hogarth's ambition to beat the French at their
own game. On the other hand he could take pride in the warm and unaffected realism of his portrait of the philanthropic sea captain, and it is an
indication of the strength of Hogarth's image that it should succeed in
bringing a distinctively English sensibility to a type of portrait associated
with quite a different world of ideas. By domesticating the French Grand
Manner portrait Hogarth made it fit for the depiction of professional men;
Captain Coram stands at the head of the great series of portraits by notable
eighteenth-century artists in the Foundling Hospital.

133

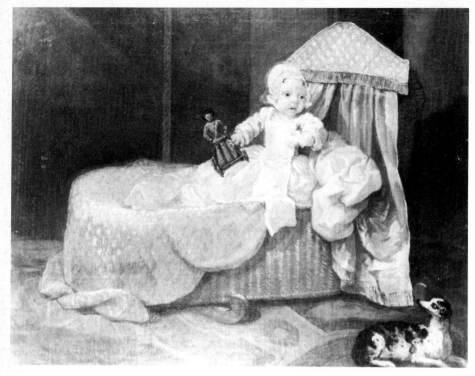

103   *Gerard Anne Edwards*, 1732

Sadly, hardly any commissions for full dress portraits came Hogarth's
way. One of the few to follow from the Coram portrait came from Mary
Edwards, a good friend, who commissioned a number of works from
106   Hogarth, including a splendid three-quarter-length portrait of herself
(Frick Collection, New York). She was reputed to be the richest woman in
England, having inherited a vast fortune in her own right, but she fell for
the rakish Scottish nobleman Lord Anne Hamilton, who after their wedding
in 1731 set about to dissipate her fortune. Their brief marriage is com-
103   memorated by Hogarth in the enchanting painting of their son Gerard
Anne in his cradle (National Trust, Upton House) and the revealing
104   conversation piece in which all three are seen on a terrace. Mary Edwards
gestures towards the child; she has open *The Spectator* at essay 580, where
Addison expatiates on the omnipresence of the Deity, illustrating movingly
her notion of her child as a sign of that omnipresence and her desire to bring

134

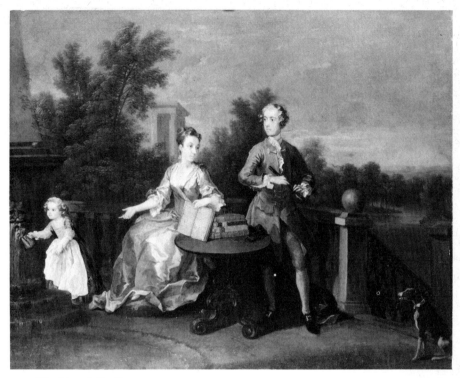

104   *The Edwards Family*, 1733–34

him up with an awareness of it. We need not doubt that she was responsible
for choosing this text and for the stirring patriotism of the letter lying on
her desk in the Frick portrait. In splendour and warmth this image is   *106*
entirely the equal of *Captain Coram*, and is as rich in symbolism. A bust of   *101*
Queen Elizabeth in the background and the globe assert Mary Edwards'
queenly stoutheartedness. There is no precedent in Hogarth's work, or
indeed in English portraiture, for the emphatic richness of her red dress
which is laid against a green drape, and the vigorous plasticity of the details
of the ruffles and fob watch. By the time the picture was painted, 1742, Miss
Edwards had long annulled her marriage to the feckless Lord Anne and had
taken her affairs into her own hands. Like *Captain Coram* this great portrait
was the fruit of friendship and admiration on Hogarth's part, and it gives
cause for regret that there were not more such friends with the means to
commission grand portraits.

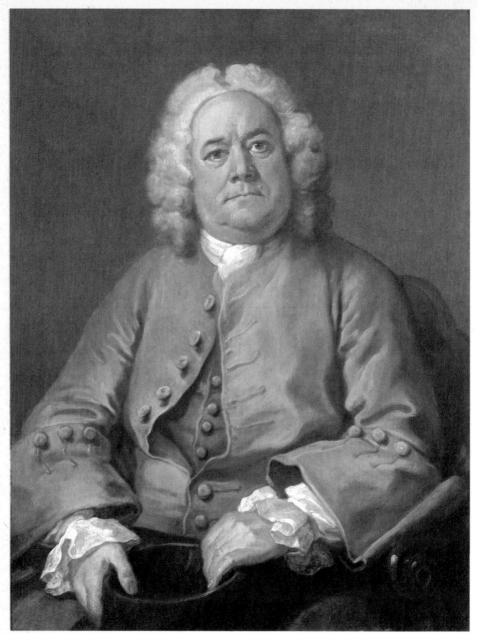

105   *George Arnold, c.* 1740

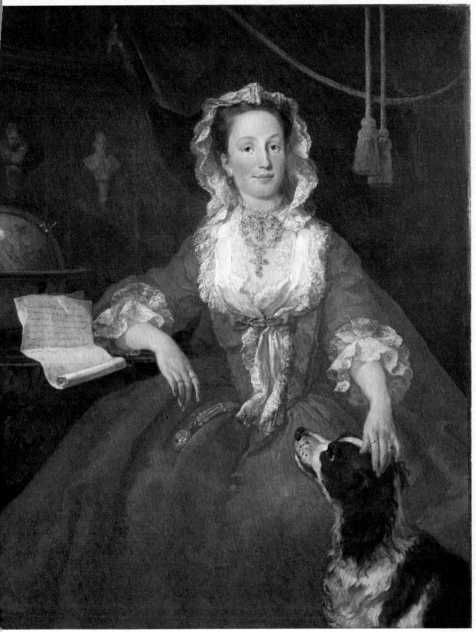

106   *Miss Mary Edwards*, 1742

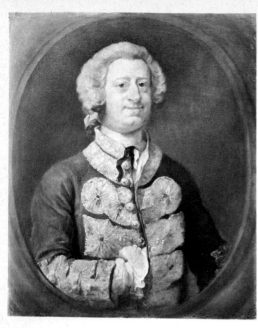

107 *William James, c.* 1740–45

Hogarth painted a large number of half-length portraits in the early 1740s, and it is at this point that he comes closest to his professional colleagues. Many of them are quite dull, but occasionally he does break free and produce something almost startling in its individuality, even dangerously near to caricature. One can scarcely imagine anyone wanting to be depicted

107 with such comical rubicundity as William James (Worcester Art Museum, Mass.), yet Hogarth's determined directness could also produce such a

105 masterpiece of middle-class rectitude as *George Arnold* (Fitzwilliam Museum, Cambridge), a painting which is to the eighteenth-century merchant what Ingres' *M. Bertin* was to his French nineteenth-century equivalent.

Because Hogarth was very rarely if ever able to obtain commissions outside his circle of acquaintances, he was also more likely to attract patrons who wanted unusual portraits for special purposes. On occasions he may also have entered into a portrait as a speculative venture, as in the case of

108 *David Garrick as Richard III* (Walker Art Gallery, Liverpool). In fact this is hardly a portrait at all, and one could equally regard it as a History painting growing out of his attempts at the Grand Manner in the 1730s. In its mixing of genres it was prophetic of two later developments in British art of the latter part of the century: the literary painting in the Grand Manner of subjects from Shakespeare or Milton, and the large-scale portrait which employs the conventions of History to add dignity and drama to the por-

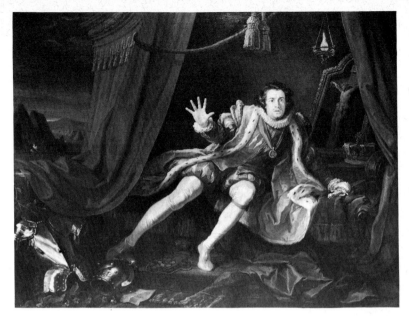

108   *David Garrick as Richard III*, 1745

trayal of an eminent person. Hogarth seems not to have been commissioned by Garrick, but to have made this very large picture (it is over 8 feet, some 2·5 m, long) with some connivance from the publicity-seeking actor, for both had much to gain from the painting's success. It spawned no real progeny in his own work, and again only with a later generation, that of Johann Zoffany (1733?–1810) who came to England in 1760, did the genre of theatrical portrait become fully established, with Garrick again as the key figure.

Another unusual commission, this time one which had apparently no precedent or progeny, was the portrait of Frank Matthew Schutz (Private Collection). It appears to have been commissioned by Schutz's wife on their marriage to warn him that his days of dissipation were over. (An inscription on the floor, from one of Horace's *Odes*, tells us that a man over forty need no longer be suspected.) Schutz is seen leaning out of bed, a very sickly figure, reading a letter: according to family tradition before the picture was altered by a squeamish descendant he was vomiting into a basin instead. Despite the potentially disgusting subject it is painted with the utmost delicacy and beauty. Equally perverse is the portrait of Sir Francis Dashwood (Private Collection), at his highly blasphemous devotions: the artist has wittily subverted a seventeenth-century type of hermit saint for his image of the most notorious member of the rakish Hellfire Club.

109

110

139

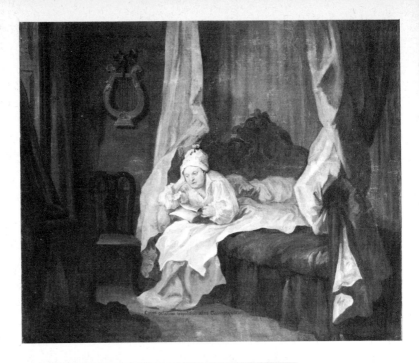

109 *Frank Matthew Schutz, c. 1755–60*

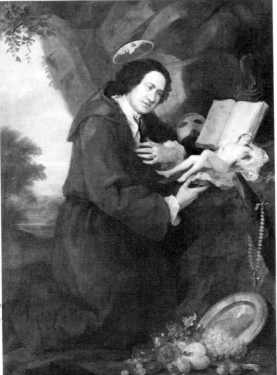

110 *Sir Francis Dashwood at his Devotions, 1742–46*

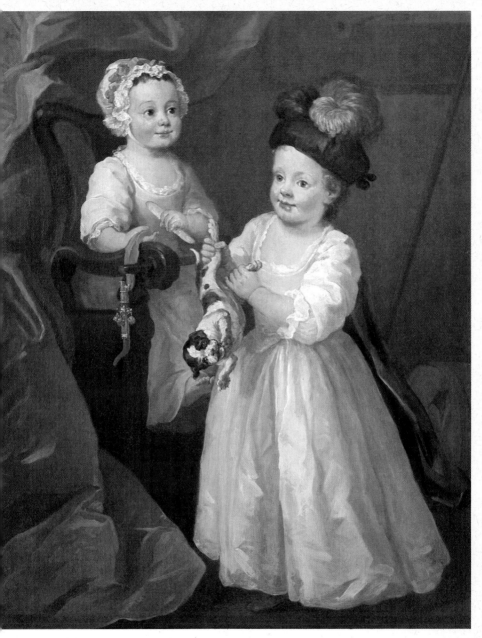

111   *Lord Grey and Lady Mary West as Children, 1740*

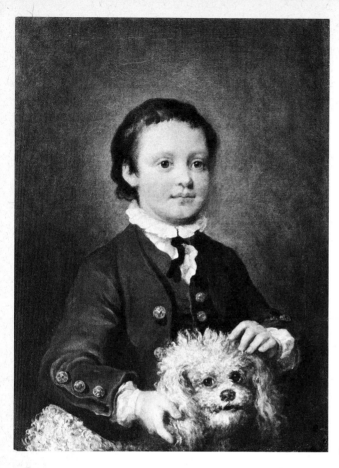

112 *Boy in a Green Coat,*
c. 1756

Hogarth's paintings of children almost represent a separate genre within his portraiture for their rare sympathy and freshness. They capture the seriousness of childish pursuits without being sentimental, yet they express subtly a number of distinctively eighteenth-century notions: that childhood is a transient state, that children seek instinctively to imitate adults, and that their affectionate nature can coexist with thoughtless cruelty. The
112 frankness of gaze of the subject in the *Boy in a Green Coat* (Art Gallery of Ontario) mimics the seriousness of adult life, while the enchanting three-
111 year-old son of the 5th Earl of Stamford, whose year-old sister is seated behind him, thoughtlessly holds a pathetically struggling puppy by its hind legs (Washington University, St Louis). All these themes are sub-

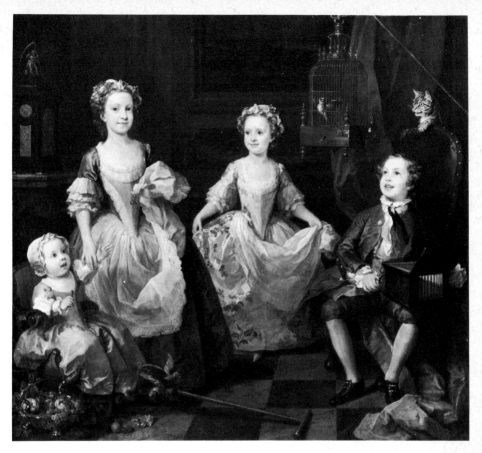

113   *The Graham Children*, 1742

sumed within the large group of *The Graham Children* (Tate Gallery), one   *113, 114*
of the definitive accounts of eighteenth-century childhood. Nothing in
previous portraiture equals the subtlety with which Hogarth differentiates
the ages and personalities of these children. The eldest girl is self-consciously
motherly in her solemn expression and the responsible way in which she
restrains the youngest child on her cart, and she may be contrasted with the
open sunniness of her younger siblings. Yet there are profound themes here
as well and Hogarth indicates the passing of time and youthful innocence in
a number of ways. There is an element of instability in the painting; an
impending breakage or collapse which provides a poetic image of the
passing of childhood and human life. A clock with a scythe-carrying

143

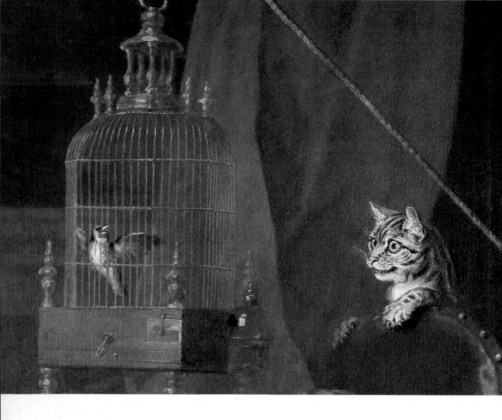

Cupid is prominently displayed on the left, but the dramatic pivot of the
painting is the defiantly ordinary cat which is terrifying the goldfinch in
its cage, making it utter cries which the boy in his innocence takes as happy
warbling to his music box. The infant on the left is reaching for the cherries
(or may have observed the cat) but is restrained by its eldest sister. The clear
grouping reminiscent of an adult conversation piece is shown to be on the
point of disarray, and behind the humour of the depiction is a theme worthy
of a History painting.

Hogarth inevitably tended to emphasize his differences from other
painters of portraits and to contrast his own independence with the servility
of the 'face painters' of the time. Recent reconsideration of English portraiture in the first half of the eighteenth century has, however, tended to
make his position less isolated and has revealed that many others were
capable of a high degree of individuality. We no longer consider Kneller to
be such a dull artist, and many other painters of the time have begun to
emerge from the dark varnish in country house corridors and reveal
themselves as considerable personalities.

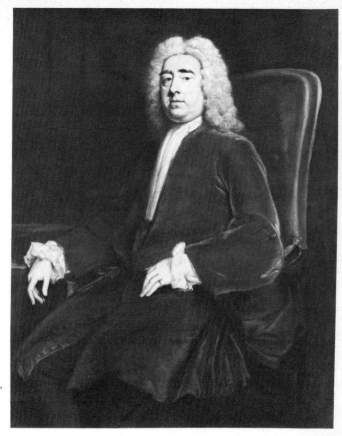

114 (opposite) Detail of
The Graham Children,
1742

115 Jonathan
Richardson:
*Francis Godolphin,
2nd Earl of
Godolphin*

Hogarth would have been familiar with the grand portraits by Thornhill, and they are reflected in his more formal portraits. Nor should one
underestimate the influence of Kneller himself, whose broad handling with
emphatic highlights and tendency to work from light to dark was his
inheritance from his master Rembrandt; and to the tradition of Rembrandt
Hogarth can in this sense, as Lawrence Gowing has pointed out, be said to
belong.

Hogarth was tied by close friendship to many of the artists, including
Jonathan Richardson (1665–1745) and Joseph Highmore, who represent the
immediate post-Kneller generation. Richardson's portrait of the 2nd Earl of   *115*
Godolphin (Yale Center for British Art, New Haven) is more static in
conception than anything by Hogarth, but it is both commanding and
elegant in execution, and his drawings of the great men in his circle like
Pope and Vertue are sensitive and warm. The closest in spirit to Hogarth in

145

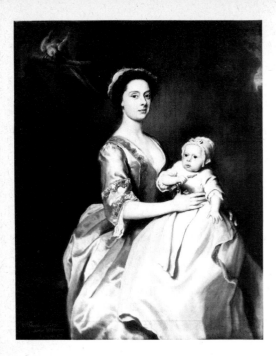

116 Joseph Highmore: *Mrs Sharp and Child*

117 (*right*) Allan Ramsay: *Alexander Boswell, Lord Auchinleck, c.* 1748–54

118 (*far right*) Sir Joshua Reynolds: *Portrait of an Unknown Man,* 1748

directness and informality is undoubtedly Highmore, who had already established a considerable practice by the early 1720s. In his large portrait of
116 1731, *Mrs Sharp and Child* (Yale Center for British Art), we see well before Hogarth was established as a portrait painter a combination of genial humanity with a Van Dyckian grandeur and elegance, and with his portrait of Charles Penruddocke of 1743 (also in the Yale Center for British Art) we are approaching the sprightliness of Hogarth's *Duke of Devonshire.*

The popularity of Vanloo was a sign of things to come, for taste by the 1740s was turning away from the impassive directness of the Hudsons and Richardsons towards a more Italianate and graceful style in which classical allusions might subtly indicate the learning of the sitter. The Scottish artist Allan Ramsay (1713–84) set up as a portraitist in 1738 in Covent Garden and quickly achieved the success he sought. Hogarth naturally was a little resentful of the painter he pointedly called 'Ramseye', but they were family friends through Ramsay's father, and the younger artist seems to have gone out of his way to be respectful towards Hogarth. Ramsay might seem to be the complete antithesis of all that Hogarth stood for: he was a placid, respectable, cultivated man with an easy social manner and a liking for smart company. His paintings are refined, with the brushwork, in the contemporary Roman manner, concealed under a smooth surface (in

146

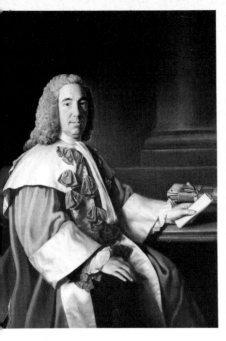
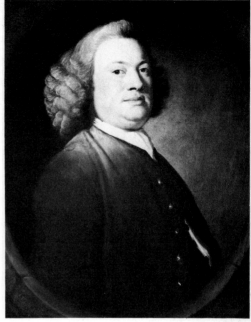

Vertue's words 'rather lick't than pencilled'). They were an instant success
with the aristocracy, particularly the Scots. To Hogarth's disgust, Ramsay   *117*
relied heavily on the drapery painter Van Aken. On the other hand he
constantly defended the 'naturalness' of Hogarth's paintings and deliberately
took the part of those who thought paintings should reach beyond the
narrow taste of the cultivated, characterizing himself in his dialogue *On
Taste* as Colonel Freeman in conversation with the fashionable Lord Modish.
And in fact it would do Ramsay a great injustice to see his paintings as
simply following the pattern of Pompeo Batoni's elegant portraits of young
aristocrats on the Grand Tour. His conception of naturalness is, however,
quite different from Hogarth's; his best works are 'natural' in the cultivated
sense of the French and Scottish Enlightenment, often depicting people who
saw naturalness as a rejection of pomp and who sought to combine ease of
manner with intellectual seriousness. It is perhaps indicative of the limita-
tions of artistic theory in the eighteenth century that Hogarth and Ramsay
could to such a large degree share a similar theoretical position. Ramsay's
reputation had nothing to fear from Hogarth, but in the end he himself
began to lose ground in the 1750s to a younger artist, Joshua Reynolds   *118*
(1723–92), who transcended him in his intellectual appeal and yet was
capable of the manly directness of Hogarth.

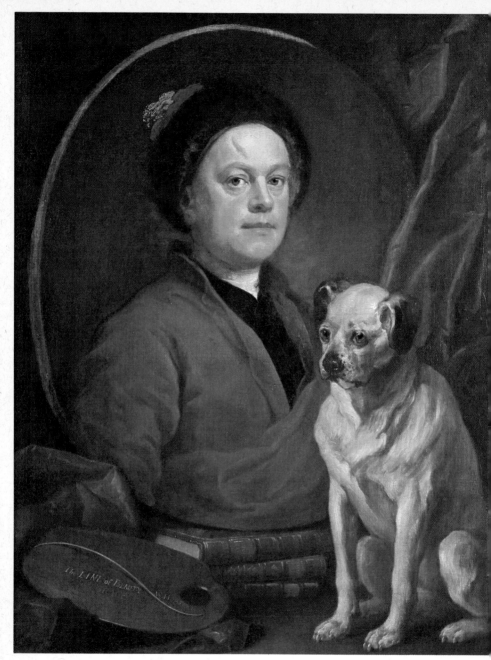

119   *The Painter and his Pug*, 1745

CHAPTER EIGHT

The Theory and Practice of Art

HOGARTH ALWAYS HAD a strong pedagogical streak, perhaps inherited from his father, and he was conscious that much of his approach to art was different from that of his contemporaries because he had in essence worked it out for himself. He had developed his method of memorizing attitude and gesture in the 1720s when he was attending the St Martin's Lane Academy, and it is to be expected that in the 1740s, when he was thinking about the genres of art, he should have contemplated a treatise about the mechanics of painting. Hogarth was passionately interested in the teaching of art, and had strong views which he attempted to put into practice when he inherited the Academy after Thornhill's death. He was opposed to any kind of hierarchy in the school, even to having a formal head and salaried professors. His continued resistance to official academies on the French model tended to isolate him from his fellow artists, who saw them as a means to achieving professional status. Like Voltaire he felt that formal academies discouraged genius, and he could point to the example of the French Academy for confirmation. He argued that in any society there could only be a dozen or so artists of any real merit, and there was an unbridgeable gap between those of 'middling talents' and true imaginative artists. He was not hostile to instruction, but he had specific views on what could be taught and what could not. The essential qualities of art, he argued, could only be acquired by observation: variety, character and expression came from nature, and they were to be learned in a way that did not inhibit the imagination. This meant that he opposed the standard method of artistic training, by endless copying of casts and Old Master paintings, which he believed could only teach the student the less important things about art. If real art was to be about real life it should concern itself with observation: the principal object of study should not be 'the stony features of a venus' but a 'blooming young girl of fifteen', an ideal embodied in his free sketch known as *The Shrimp Girl* (National Gallery).   120

In the late and unfinished manuscript in the British Library known as *The Apology for Painters*, Hogarth gave in fragmentary form his views on the place of art in society through the ages. He argued, and this is not an original view, that the art of Greece was closely connected with religion, and that

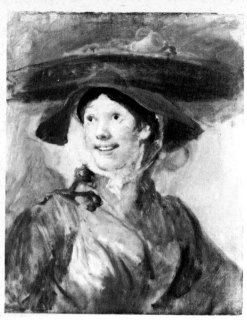

120   *The Shrimp Girl*, after 1740

Greek art 'spoke to the eye in a language every one understood'. Contrariwise such a language can no longer be appropriate to a 'trading nation'; the art of antiquity can therefore be of real interest only to dilettantes. In his pessimistic view a trading nation like England cannot support much of a market for true art, so artists should be actively discouraged from pursuing a career, lest they wish that they had instead 'been brought up cobblers'. Such a view may reflect the gloom of Hogarth's last years, when the *Apology* was written. Nonetheless it reveals the gap between his view of the world and that of his less cynical contemporaries, who thought that professional organization was the key to the rebirth of British art.

As a result, on all issues to do with artistic education Hogarth was to find himself increasingly isolated from the 1740s onwards. The move towards a Royal Academy became inexorable in that decade, and it was only the quarrelsome nature of the artists concerned that delayed its foundation until 1768. The idea of Italy, despite Hogarth's comment that to study there was an 'errant farce', was becoming ever stronger, and in the 1740s and 50s more and more English artists, including Reynolds, were beginning to make their way to Rome. Artists saw ever greater advantages in a professional association in which instruction and teaching would be on a formal and permanent basis, and in writings on art we find a continuing emphasis on learning rather than observation, and the ideal rather than 'imperfect' nature.

150

It is against this background that we need to look at Hogarth's one complete book on art, *The Analysis of Beauty*, which was published in 1753 but existed in embryo in 1745 when he painted the famous *Self-Portrait* in the Tate. That picture appears at first sight to be a notably direct portrait with a level gaze of striking candour and plainness. In fact we are really looking at a portrait within a portrait, an oval canvas resting on a pile of books. This conceit points wittily to the paradox inherent in the painting of reality, for the canvas is elegantly framed by enfolding Baroque drapes and contrasts with the 'real' and demotic form of the pug dog in the foreground. The position of the canvas within the picture also introduces the allegory, for it rests on the works of Shakespeare, Swift and Milton. Hogarth's dependence on English rather than classical authors is predictable, and the presence of Milton suggests a desire on Hogarth's part to be considered a master of the epic in painting. Balancing the pug is a palette on which there is an unexplained line labelled 'The Line of Beauty and of Grace', which as a further paradox has a shadow and thus a substance. The explanation of this reference did not appear until eight years later, in *The Analysis of Beauty*: the point, Hogarth tells us in the preface, was simply to excite curiosity, and 'The bait soon took; and no Egyptian hierogliphic ever amused more than it did for a time, painters and sculptors came to me to know the meaning of it, being as much puzzled with it as other people, till it came to have some explanation.'

The *Analysis* was probably meant as one volume in a series of which it alone reached completion. If *The Apology for Painters* is the vestige of an attempt to write a book on the purposes and social relations of art, then *The Analysis of Beauty* is the volume dealing with the aesthetic and psychological effects of painting. It is not a manual of art or purely pedagogical, nor does its bias towards the visual aspects of art mean that Hogarth regarded art as an end in itself: his own art makes it clear that questions of genre and moral purpose were equally important to him. It is true that he speaks scathingly of treatises which take the 'more beaten path of moral beauty', but his objection to them is not that they embrace such questions, but that they stop short of the real issues by falling back on phrases like 'Je ne sais quoi' or call beauty a gift from heaven. He also dislikes the connoisseurs' use of a language 'over-born by pompous terms of art', arguing that because they are concerned exclusively with works of art they do not have enough familiarity with nature to make proper judgments. If we look sympathetically upon Hogarth's attempt to define the criteria of beauty in plain terms we must also be aware of the essential loneliness of his theoretical position in the early 1750s. His determined empiricism and attempt to reduce the Beau Ideal to an observed method could hardly appeal to those influenced

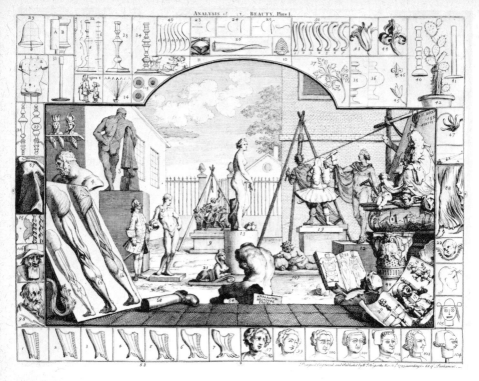

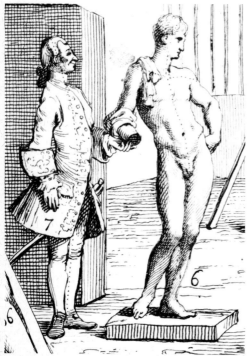

121, 122   Plate I of *The Analysis of Beauty*, engraving, 1753; *left*, detail of the dancing master and *Antinous*

123   (*opposite*) Plate II of *The Analysis of Beauty*, engraving, 1753

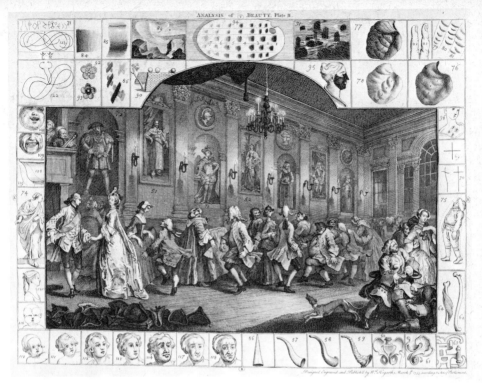

by the classical idealism of Rome. Nor could the connoisseurs, with their elevated conception of art, be really interested in a work which claimed to consider things which 'seem most to please and entertain the eye'. This is not to say, however, that Hogarth's treatise did not have influential supporters and a great impact on younger men.

A theoretical account of the *Analysis* hardly does justice to the wit and style with which Hogarth deals with potentially dry and academic issues. The book, like his prints, is deliberately not directed at those learned in the history of art. Examples are chosen as much from everyday life as from art, and they are illustrated amusingly: the idea, for example, that the joining together of discordant parts of the body provokes laughter is shown by an old man dressed up as a baby, which Hogarth had observed at St Bartholomew Fair, and the observation that the most natural and graceful posture of a man is to be slightly curved rather than straightbacked is demonstrated by a complacent dancing master standing uprightly next to the statue of *122* Antinous. Hogarth conflated all the visual illustrations to his argument into two large plates. The first depicts a sculptor's yard filled with a wide *121* variety of classical and modern sculptures, while the second shows a country dance, an adaptation of one of his *Happy Marriage* designs with *123, 127*

153

illustrative paintings on the walls: one plate displays mainly works of art, and the other unidealized humanity, but the principles apply equally to both.

Hogarth's primary idea is that the true standard of beauty is set by nature, not by art, however admirable. The true connoisseur, then, must be a man of observation and not blinkered by art alone: 'Who but a bigot, even to the antiques, will say that he has not seen faces and necks, hands and arms, in living women, that even the Grecian Venus doth but coarsely imitate?' The chief source of delight in nature is variety and this applies equally to a work of art. Intricacy of effect is particularly pleasing, for it 'leads the eye a wanton kind of chace'. This notion is based upon a knowledge of the eye's limited field of vision and the empathy between the eye's movement and the movement in nature; in Hogarth's simile an eye observing a dancing woman 'was dancing with her all the time'. Hogarth reduces these notions of variety and empathy to a basic line, a serpentine curve which can be observed equally in art and nature and is at the basis of all beautiful forms. This is the 'line of beauty', and in the accompanying plates there are a vast number of witty comparisons between things which conform and deviate in varying degrees from the ideal curve, from corsets to chairlegs.

Hogarth's target is the classical idea that true beauty is dependent on simplicity and the symmetry of the parts. He argues that simplicity is not a primary quality, but one that may be required to temper excess, for 'Simplicity, without variety, is wholly insipid.' His attacks on regularity and uniformity are expressed in revealing examples. In architecture he praises St Paul's and calls Wren 'the prince of architects', contrasting his work with the uniformity of the Palladian style, claiming with some justice that 'were a modern architect to build a palace in Lapland, or the West-Indies, Palladio must be his guide, nor would he dare stir a step without it'. In a stroke of fancy he proposes that each type of building, whether it be church, palace or prison, should have its own order, and that capitals, instead of tamely following the classical orders, should look again at natural forms. Then, characteristically, he deflates his own idea by proposing a capital for law courts 'composed of the aukward and confin'd forms of hats and periwigs' (plate I, 48). Most importantly, however, his search for variety led him to reconsider as subjects for appreciation phenomena which were almost completely alien to his time: his recognition of the 'pleasing kind of horror' of large rocks, and his delight in the romantic prospect of Windsor Castle make him an important precursor of the taste for the Sublime and Gothic.

The Analysis of Beauty, like all such treatises, is a contribution to a debate and an answer to previous arguments. Vertue tells us that as early as 1745

121

'Hogarth (in opposition to Hussey['s] scheme of Triangles) much comments on the inimitable curve or beauty of the S undulating motion line'. We have already come across Giles Hussey as a characteristic pet of the connoisseurs, who said the right kind of things, but never actually completed any serious works of art. According to Vertue Hussey claimed that all the great antique sculptures were faulty in some way, and he had found the secret of perfect proportion by a method of trigonometry which he had only imparted to a few people. In particular he found the Farnese Hercules to be defective, and it may not be coincidental that Hogarth defends it at some length in the *Analysis* (plate I, 3). There can be no doubt that Hogarth would have known about Hussey's theories and would have regarded him, not quite fairly, as the kind of pedant who spends his time measuring antique statues, and finds that the left leg of the Apollo Belvedere is a fraction longer than the right, without any understanding of it as a work of art. *121*

Just as Reynolds was to have to suffer the widespread imputation that he did not write the *Discourses*, so Hogarth had to bear complaints that he was not the real author of the *Analysis*. He certainly had extensive help from learned friends, particularly the Rev. Thomas Morell, the interpreter of Locke. Hogarth's own manuscript drafts are a scholar's nightmare, without punctuation or coherence, and there can be no doubt that the clarity of the final product and some of the wide-ranging learning was due to his friends. On the other hand, the main ideas were certainly his own, as was the wonderful sense of observation. Equally some of the eccentricities were his, like the denial of elegance to Van Dyck, an opinion we know infuriated the portrait painters he encountered at coffee houses. As Joseph Burke has pointed out, it is significant that Hogarth should have found more support from a circle of rational divines and doctors than from his fellow artists. These men, learned in empirical philosophy and science, would have encouraged his predilection for observation and the evidence of the senses, in preference to inherited wisdom.

In the *Country Dance* plate of the *Analysis* Hogarth provides samples of *123* perfect elegance in, for example, the couple to the left, and in one of the marginal diagrams (no. 71) this couple and all the others in the dance are reduced to their linear equivalent, their relative elegance depending upon their reduction to straight or curved lines. Thus the obviously inelegant figure of the small man immediately to the right of the elegant lady is shown to be reducible to a diamond shape. Now this method must relate ultimately to Hogarth's system of remembering attitudes that he observed in the street, which was to reduce them essentially to linear figures which *20* could be reconstituted in the studio.

155

124, 125 (*overleaf*) The boy piper and the brothel, from *The March to Finchley*, 1746 (see ill. 126)

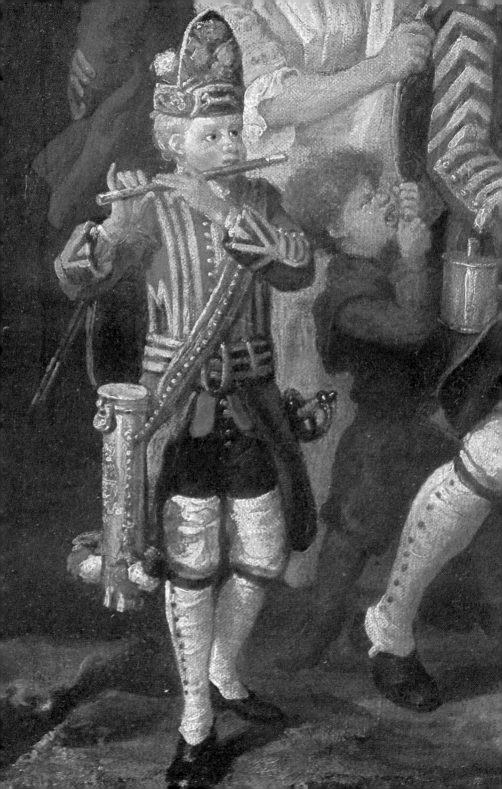

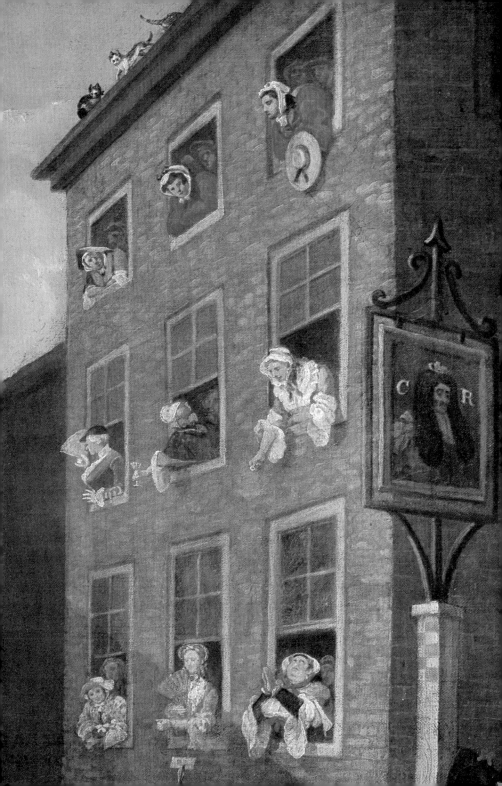

Hogarth was never very explicit about his memory system and he did not publish his method. One reason for his reticence might have lain in his, and Fielding's, definition of caricature as the exaggeration of a single feature of the human body. In the print of *The Bench* Hogarth points out that 'the humourous Effects of the fashionable manner of Caracaturing chiefly depend on the surprize we are under at finding ourselves caught with any sort of Similitude in objects absolutely remote in their kind', and he gives as an example 'a famous Caracatura of a certain Italian Singer, that Struck at first sight, which consisted only of a Streight perpendicular Stroke with a Dot over it'. Hogarth's method of linear shorthand was, therefore, dangerously near to being a form of caricature, and he knew that the connoisseurs would be likely to leap upon such an apparent contradiction.

The question must be asked: does the *Analysis* shed any light on Hogarth's practice as a painter? To a certain extent obviously it does, but the relationship between theory and practice is not straightforward at all levels. To take an example from the Countess's Morning Levée in *Marriage-a-la-Mode*, the figures of the dancing master and the singer correspond precisely to his notion of the inelegant, the former being very thin and made up almost entirely of straight lines while the latter is excessively fat and curvilinear. Yet they are dressed fashionably, while the Countess, whose attitude generally corresponds to the line of beauty, is still *en deshabillé*. In the first painting, the Marriage Contract, the heir, preening himself foppishly, adopts a linear shape that is almost a diamond, while the old Earl's adoption of an elegant serpentine attitude is spoiled by his pot-belly and gouty foot. Many of Hogarth's satirical strokes at the polite world are sharpened by the visual effect of straight and serpentine lines, and this can also be seen in such comic low-life pictures as *The March to Finchley* of 1746 (Thomas Coram Foundation for Children), where bestiality and stupidity are shown in overwhelming profusion. Here there is a contrast, as with fops and musician, between the gorgeousness of the soldiers' uniforms and their gross attitudes; true beauty is only to be found in the youthful fifer, whose intense concentration and graceful attitude provide a note of youthful innocence among the horrors of the adult world.

On the other hand, while Hogarth's system of memory and his theory of beauty are essentially linear his way of painting is not. It is bold and painterly from the beginning of his career, and his concern is with shape rather than contour. A linear structure may dictate the overall form of a figure, but the outline flows without regularity, just as a Baroque sculptor might make the drapery billow out in opposition to the direction of the figure. Hogarth's method is therefore not a reductive one, but can incorporate additional elements almost indefinitely, and allow endless ramifica-

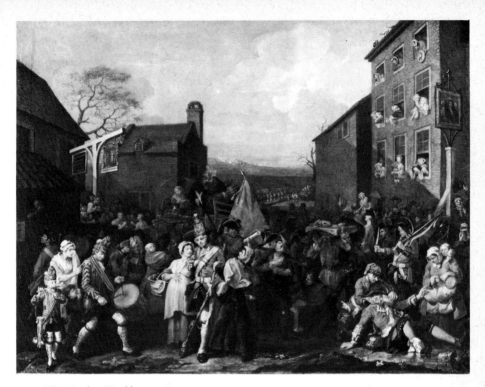

126 *The March to Finchley*, 1746

tions to follow from a particular action. Once the attitude of the figure has been caught there is no limit to the expressive details which may be added to complete the effect, nor to the additional elements which may be brought into a composition. In the Countess's Levée the dancing master is defined   *76* by his posture and his character is enriched by telling touches: his hair is in curlers, he sips effeminately from the cup, and his hand on his stomach suggests delicate health. To the classical argument that such extraneous detail only detracts from the clarity of the story Hogarth could reply that the delight which is given to the spectator by such variety would be an inducement for him to work out the story himself. Furthermore the application of the serpentine line to the overall composition links the figures to   *82* each other and keeps the eye moving from the Italian singer to the lawyer Silvertongue and the screen behind him, and implicitly to the *dénouement* in   *83* the next painting.

From his earliest years Hogarth tended to build the composition according to a sequence which begins with a relatively minor incident on the left, through a serpentine path to a culminating incident on the right – a method,

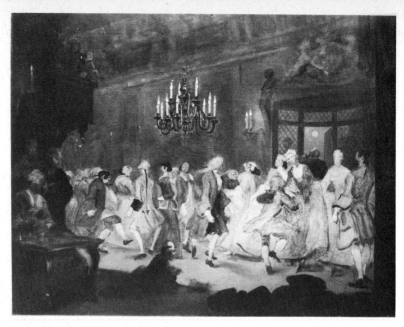

127, 128   *The Wedding Dance, c.* 1745

57, 65 incidentally, which can be disrupted by the engraving being in reverse from the painting. If one compares, say, the Levée in *The Rake's Progress* with the 50, 82 Countess's Levée it becomes clear how much more graceful Hogarth's later compositions are, and we need not doubt that his reflections on composition in the *Analysis* were prompted by his experience of working the problems out on canvas.

There are, however, other developments in Hogarth's method of painting which cannot be accounted for by reference to his theory. From the few unfinished paintings that have survived it is evident that Hogarth's method of laying in his ground gradually changed, and that over the years he was becoming more sensitive to the overall painterly effect. The un- 127, 128 finished painting of *The Wedding Dance* (South London Art Gallery, on loan to the Tate Gallery), from the *Happy Marriage* series, shows that his primary concern was to establish the space and, as it is a night scene, the relationship between light and dark. The chandeliers are the most completely finished part, and their light contrasts with the soft light of the moon, which hauntingly illuminates the bald head of a man mopping his brow at the open window. Hogarth has brushed in the attitudes of the dancers very freely and has indicated their individual colours while still

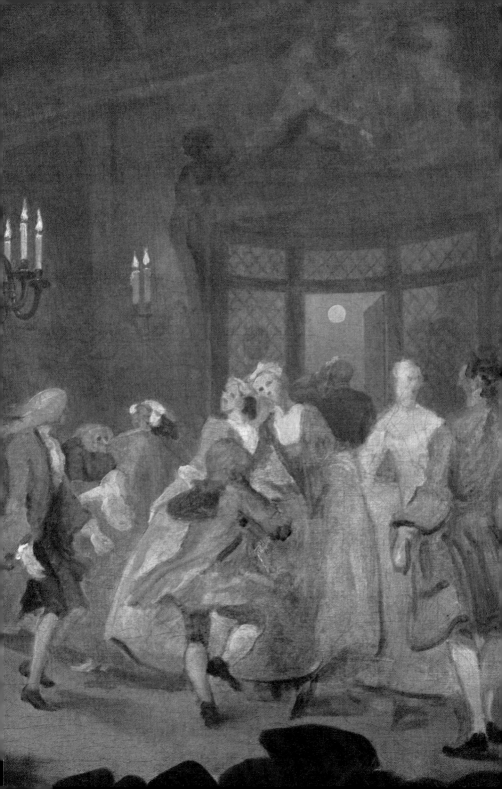

preserving the overall harmony. From this example and others we can see that Hogarth in the 1740s aimed to keep each part of the painting in a comparable state of finish so that the interrelationship of tone and colour could be balanced to the end. Outline plays virtually no part in the construction, but only broad strokes of the brush, which become paste-like for the white highlights.

24   A comparison between *The Beggar's Opera* of 1729 and *Calais Gate, or*
129–131   *The Roast Beef of Old England* of 1748 (Tate Gallery) shows an enormous development in Hogarth's mastery of form. The former is no less lively in handling but the figures have little solidity and do not fit comfortably in space; in the latter, on the other hand, the contrast between bulk and thinness in the human figures, which makes an important satirical point, is made much more real, and some parts of the picture have a Chardin-like plasticity.
131   The clarity and weight of such details as the soup pail carried by the scrawny French soldiers suggest that Hogarth could have been a great still-life painter, and indeed in the 1740s one becomes conscious of a discrepancy between the mordancy of his view of human nature and the opulence of his
130   painterly technique. The view through the Calais Gate in *The Roast Beef of Old England* shows the Host being administered to the sick while the dove of the Holy Ghost appears on a pub sign above, but it is depicted with such beauty of handling that the crudely satirical point is almost lost. In *The*
126   *March to Finchley* the drunken and dissolute rabble are painted with a disconcerting fineness, and the sunlit glimpse of Hampstead in the background is radiantly at odds with the foreground.

Hogarth's bold use of colour represents another way in which he stood out against the connoisseurs, who tended to regard colour as a secondary attribute of art, because it was resistant to rules and therefore unteachable. Jonathan Richardson and others, and indeed Hogarth, held that only a few artists had ever achieved greatness as colourists. Hogarth applied his principle of variety to colouring and argued that 'the utmost beauty of colouring depends on the great principle of varying all the means of varying, and on the proper and artful union of that variety'. Richardson in general took a similar view, implicitly seeing such variety as a lesser object of ambition for the painter. Hogarth did not go so far as to see colour as solely a matter of science, but he did attack the mystery with which the connoisseurs had surrounded colour, and it is likely that he was more familiar with Newton's discoveries, through his circle of friends and particularly Dr Morell, than most of his fellow painters.

The originality of Hogarth's ideas lies in his claim that there is no limit to the brilliance that an artist can and should achieve: he was unmoved by the example of darkened Old Masters, or the idea that paintings should be

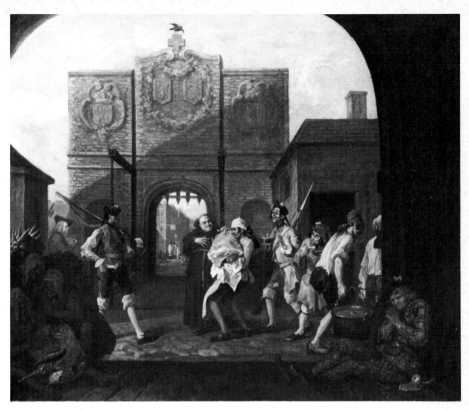

129   *Calais Gate, or The Roast Beef of Old England*, 1748

reticent in the name of propriety. The tints, especially in the flesh, should be
kept distinct from each other and the artist should avoid an effect whereby
colours are 'smoothed and absolutely blended together'. This can be
observed in Hogarth's practice, as he frequently intensifies the vitality of
effect by placing contrasting colours next to each other with the aim of
making 'the distinction of the parts . . . more perfect'. Two figures embrac-
ing or conversing are almost always dressed in contrasting colours, and this
principle of contrast is often observed within one figure. In the large painting of *Moses brought to Pharaoh's Daughter*, a striking effect is achieved by   *88*
making the child Moses' garment a rich olive-green with a red drape,
while Pharaoh's daughter has a pink overgarment on a white dress. The
effect is to dramatize the touching relationship between the two main
actors and push the others into the background, and it is achieved with

163

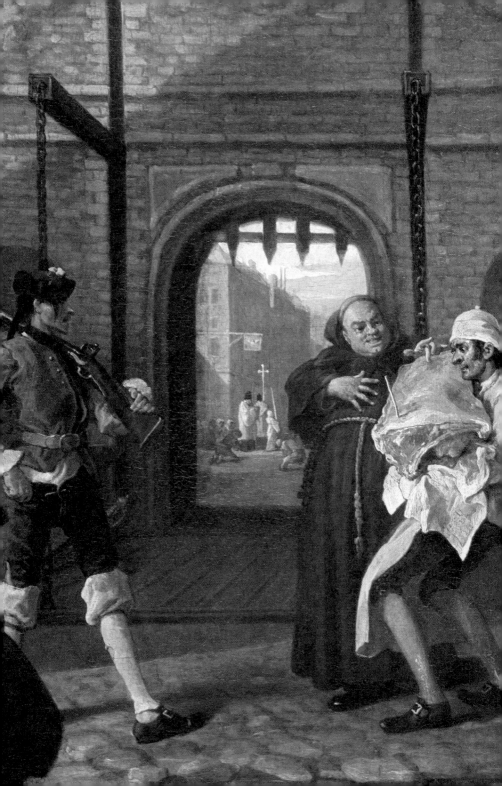

simple bold effects appropriate to a History painting. In *The March to Finchley*, on the other hand, a great range of contrasts of colour can be observed, particularly in the virtuoso painting of the soldiers' uniforms. Although the effect is riotously colourful, as befits the subject, Hogarth uses a surprisingly limited palette: yellow, red and blue are predominant, but they frequently clash boldly together. Great play is also made with tonal effects and the use of a vivid highlight which emerges from the darkness. The most powerful example is in the scene of the Earl's death in *Marriage-a-la-Mode*; the handle of his abandoned sword stuck in the floor catches the stray lights to glow in the dark with a ghastly poignancy.

124, 125

85

Experience of Hogarth's paintings only increases one's admiration for his mastery of colour. It comes as a shock, therefore, to realize that virtually no one in the eighteenth century gave him any credit for it. His paintings were woefully undervalued compared to his engravings. When he held an auction to sell his paintings in 1751 Vertue tells us 'he puffd this in news papers for a long time before hand. but alass when the time came – . . . he found himself neglected. for instead of 500 or 600 pounds he expected. there was but one person he had got to bid . . . the only sum of 120 pounds.' He could take some comfort from the reception of the *Analysis*, which, on the whole, was taken seriously by most critics and was well publicized. However, such a public statement of belief had its dangers in a polemical age, and his presumption was belaboured unmercifully by caricaturists, like Paul Sandby, who made it appear that he had slandered every great artist of the past to glorify his own art.

130, 131   Details of *Calais Gate, or The Roast Beef of Old England*, 1748

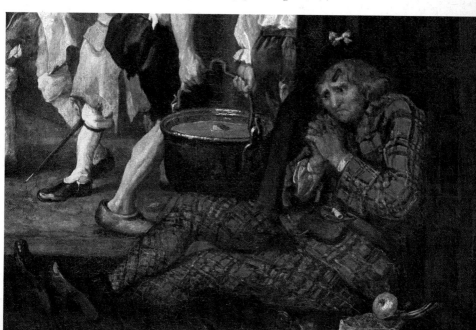

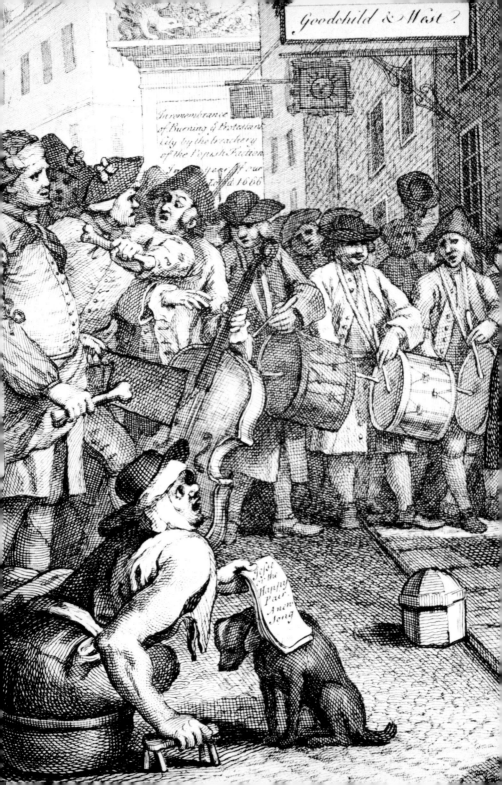

Goodchild & West?

In remembrance
of Burning & Protestant
City by the treachery
of the Popish Faction
In the year of our
Lord 1666

Jolst
of the
Happy
Pair
A new
Song

CHAPTER NINE

Approaches to the Public

HOGARTH'S RETURN to Modern Moral Subjects with the *Marriage-a-la-Mode* series in the early 1740s led him to reflect more on the potential audience for his art, which he saw as belonging outside the narrow circle of the connoisseurs. In attempting a 'benevolent' sequel to the *Marriage* he revealed a desire to go beyond the negative premises of satire, which exposes the folly and knavery of humanity, and to provide instead *exempla* of human conduct, to make his art 'useful' in a way that it had never been before. Two assumptions behind Hogarth's earlier satire were that the audience would enjoy the works and by entering into them would learn the folly of their ways; and that, no matter how particularized the circumstances, the follies and vices satirized were universal ones, like greed, idleness and gullibility. It is true that the *Marriage-a-la-Mode* series attacked the contemporary expedient of the arranged marriage, from which in a sense the human tragedy stems, but the weight of the satire rests on the more general failings of the privileged classes. By contrast the *Industry and Idleness* series of 1747, of engravings only, represented a new departure based on a different conception of the moral series: here Hogarth provides a prescription for a specific class of person, the young London apprentice, and the roads to success and failure are laid out clearly. He sought by all possible means to make the pictures as intelligible as possible, and kept the engraving simple so that 'the purchase of them became within the reach of those for whom they [were] chiefly intended'.

 This stark conception of the utility of art must be seen in the light of Hogarth's activity as a philanthropist and governor of hospitals and charities. The age of latitudinarianism was also the great age of philanthropy. The corollary to the distrust of mystery and the emphasis on works over faith of Hogarth and his friends was a belief that man had an active duty to promote the Kingdom of God on earth. Cruelty and human misery could not be treated with resignation but required to be eliminated on both humane and utilitarian grounds. Thus the great philanthropic schemes of the early eighteenth century, which led to the reform of prisons and the establishment of hospitals and orphanages, were initiated in the belief that an active man could make important improvements in society, with benefit to the improver's soul and the wealth of the nation.

1, 132,
134–140

132 Musicians and beggar, from plate 6 of *Industry and Idleness*, engraving, 1747 (see ill. 136)

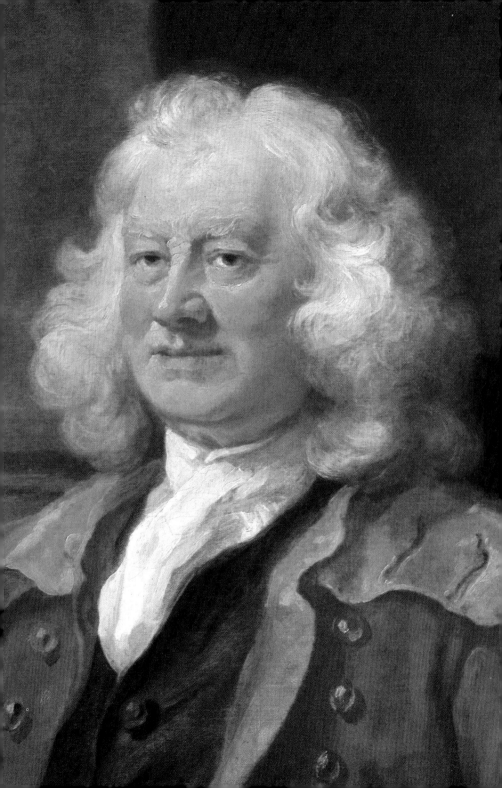

As Paulson has pointed out, Hogarth was associated in one way or another with all the great philanthropic schemes of the age, and he was especially active in the affairs of the Foundling Hospital, of which he was a founding Governor in 1739. The Foundling Hospital was the creation of Thomas Coram, a retired naval officer who had been appalled at the sight 101, 133 of so many abandoned children in the streets of London, with no future but petty crime and an early death. With the help of donations from the wealthy, the new Hospital was to educate the foundlings to become seamen and apprentices – useful Christian citizens who would occupy the subordinate positions in society. Hogarth was in total sympathy with Coram's mixture of compassion and practicality; he not only made large donations to the Hospital, but he and his wife became foster parents to some of the children. He also organized the display and donation of paintings to the Hospital, which became one of the first places where a selection of work by British artists was permanently on view. Judging by the subjects of the paintings in the Great Room, all of which are concerned with charity, Hogarth and his friends were aiming them at potential donors rather than the foundlings themselves.

The *Industry and Idleness* series can, therefore, be seen on one level as a direct response to the problems presented by the education of foundlings, whose minds, being a *tabula rasa* in the sense defined by the philosopher Locke, were to be filled with ideas of benevolence. Neither the Industrious nor the Idle Apprentice appears to have a father, and the only parent to appear is the ineffectual mother of the idle one. By being apprenticed to a manufacturer they are forced from an early age to choose their own path without parental admonition, which is in effect provided by the prints themselves. Apart from the visual form taken by Hogarth's prints there is nothing new in the theme or in general in the manner of telling. The story of two London apprentices, one of whom by industry becomes a rich City merchant while the other after a youth of idleness takes to crime, follows closely a popular play, *The London Merchant* by George Lillo (1693–1739), first published in 1731. Hogarth's knowledge of the play is proven, if it needed to be, by the fact that on a preliminary drawing for the series he identified the Idle Apprentice as Barnwell, the name of Lillo's villain. *The London Merchant*, like *Pamela*, was written by a successful small businessman in the City, and it reflects precisely the anti-aristocratic ethic we might expect, and the fear that upper-class idleness might also infect the lower orders. In the preface Lillo expresses the view that tragedy should in the first place be useful, and that its value is in no way diluted either by the large size of the audience or by the inferior social station of the protagonists: 'tragedy is so far from losing its dignity, by being accommodated to the

169

circumstances of the generality of mankind, that it is more truly august in proportion to the extent of its influence, and the numbers that are properly affected by it.'

The engravings for *Industry and Idleness* are consciously simplified to reach the 'generality of mankind', and to enable Hogarth to lower the price and make the story more comprehensible to those out of touch with the polite world. In these respects, then, they make a deliberate contrast with *Marriage-a-la-Mode*, whose intricacy of design, subtlety of reference and fine French engraving direct it towards the well-educated. In *Industry and Idleness* everything is reduced to stark moral alternatives and the range of reference is kept to a minimum, eschewing the kind of wit which depends upon a knowledge of Old Master paintings. According to Vertue the plates were executed in a 'slight poor strong manner', but in fact they are models of clear vigorous engraving, with many subtleties of handling that are lost in the infinite number of reprintings and piracies which followed their publication.

This very simplicity has, however, presented a problem to Hogarth's interpreters, for the inexorable destiny which pursues both the Idle and Industrious Apprentices to their ordained ends is hard to reconcile with what we know of Hogarth's own personality. Could he really have sympathized with a calculating prig like the Industrious Apprentice, whose life is a succession of safe choices and instant rewards? Put in such terms the answer must be negative, but this is not quite the point. Surely Hogarth was entirely in earnest in seeking to 'improve' the morals of apprentices, whom he would have regarded as children in need of exhortation and guidance. It is true that he frequently talked with bravura about his own idleness, which he claimed made him unfit for the profession of engraving, but that kind of idleness was quite different from the kind he castigates in the figure of Tom Idle. Protestations of idleness were common in the eighteenth century, for they evoked the ideal of the Latin poets who placed a life of thought above that of action. Such was not the idleness which turned into a life of petty crime.

The processional nature of the two apprentices' progress is reflected in the rigorous system of contrasts carried through the twelve plates. The two apprentices are paired together in the first plate and then go their separate ways, each episode being contrasted until they meet again in the tenth plate, one as a magistrate, the other as a felon, about to go their separate ways to Guildhall and to Tyburn. Their progress is, as in the earlier moral series, a geographical one, but in keeping with mercantile morality it is confined mainly to the City and its adjoining parishes. The Industrious Apprentice (who is called Goodchild), by a modest and pleasing demeanor

134

138

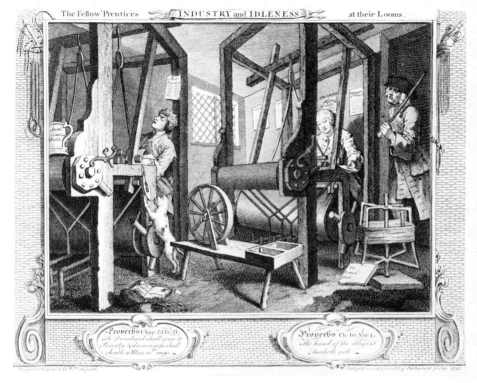

Proverbs Chap. 23 Ver. 21.
The Drunkard shall come to Poverty & drowsiness shall cloath a Man w.th rags.

Proverbs Ch. 10 Ver. 4.
The hand of the diligent maketh rich.

134   *Industry and Idleness*, 1: 'The Fellow 'Prentices at their Looms', engraving, 1747

makes a steady progress through the institutions of the City until, like Dick Whittington, he is made Lord Mayor of London. He begins as an apprentice weaver in Spitalfields, worships at what appears to be a City church (it is usually identified as St Martin-in-the-Fields but there is no evidence for that), and after promotion within the workshop in which he began sets himself up in substantial but modest style with his employer's daughter in a street by the Monument, which commemorates the Great Fire of London. Hogarth has deliberately copied the distasteful inscription on the Monument ascribing the burning of London to 'the Popish Faction', something his apologists have often tried to claim was meant ironically, but it is perfectly likely that in the aftermath of the '45 Rebellion, when the Scots rose in support of a Catholic pretender to the throne, he would wish to

134

136

132

171

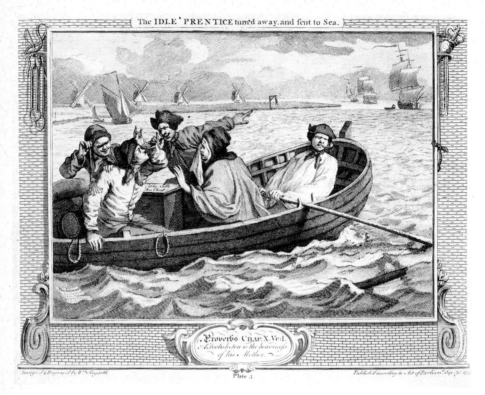

135 *Industry and Idleness*, 5: 'The Idle 'Prentice turn'd away, and sent to Sea', engraving, 1747

contrast the destructive nature of Catholicism with the constructiveness of the Protestant rebuilders of the City after the Fire. Goodchild's wealth and position as Sheriff of London are affirmed at a grand banquet, probably at Fishmongers' Hall. Finally, his apotheosis as Lord Mayor is depicted at the

140 symbolic moment when his carriage leaves St Paul's Churchyard to go along Cheapside towards the Guildhall; thus, sanctified by the Church and blessed by the presence of royalty (looking down from a balcony at the right) he moves towards the benign seat of power.

By contrast the Idle Apprentice's progress is more like a Road to Calvary.

134 After idling his time in the Spitalfields workshop he is caught gambling on a tombstone outside a City church, no doubt the same one attended by Goodchild. While Goodchild makes a short and straight journey from the

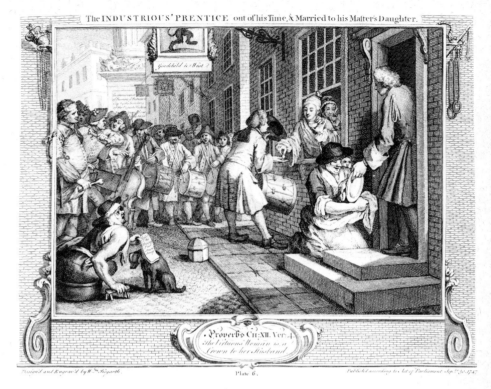

136 *Industry and Idleness*, 6: 'The Industrious 'Prentice out of his Time, & Married to his Master's Daughter', engraving, 1747

shop-floor to the counting-house, Idle escapes to a life at sea, and is seen   *135*
passing the infamous spot called Cuckold's Point, which has, prophetically,
a gibbet on the shore. His erratic journey resumes in a disgusting garret,
possibly in St Giles or in one of the insalubrious parishes to the north of the
City, like Cripplegate, in the company of a diseased prostitute, contrasting
with Goodchild's mansion and his adoring wife. The grandeur of the   *136*
Fishmongers' Hall is paired with Idle's next stop, a notorious 'night cellar'   *137*
identified by the late eighteenth-century collector Samuel Ireland as the
Blood Bowl House, between Fleet Street and the Thames near the banks
of the stinking Fleet River, where he is arrested for theft. After the enforced
meeting of the two former apprentices in a City court, Tom Idle is sent off   *138*
to Newgate Prison, whence he makes his final journey to Tyburn watched

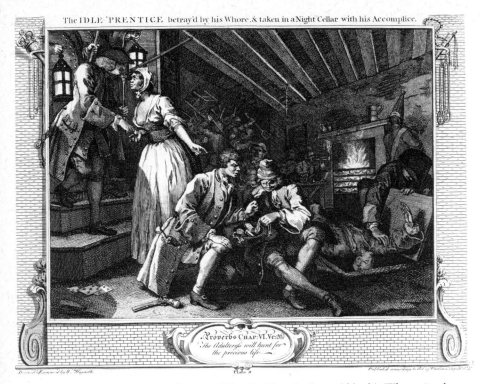

Proverbs Chap: VI. Ve: 26
The Adulteress will hunt for
the precious life.

Designed & Engraved by W. Hogarth.   Plate 9   Published according to Act of Parliam. Sep. 30. 1747

137 *Industry and Idleness*, 9: 'The Idle 'Prentice betray'd by his Whore, & taken in a Night Cellar with his Accomplice', engraving, 1747

139 by almost the whole populace of London. In the final plate, after the ghastly
140 ritual of Tyburn comes the rich contrast of the Lord Mayor's Procession;
the temporary nature of the gibbet and the presence of religious Enthusiasts
is set against the permanence of the physical structure of the City. Religion
is represented by the majestic bulk of St Paul's Cathedral rather than by the
hysterically pointing finger of the Methodist in the tumbrel with the
condemned man.

These simple polarities give the series the character of a ballad. For the
134 Industrious Prentice the tale is of the kind alluded to in the first plate by the
broadside of Dick Whittington, the medieval apprentice who became Lord
Mayor of London, on the wall behind his loom. The Idle Apprentice has
instead a broadside of Moll Flanders; but his career is perhaps more

174

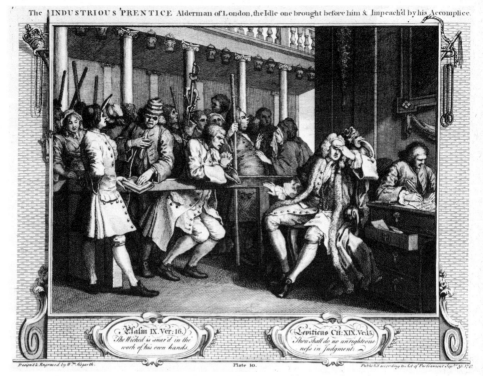

The INDUSTRIOUS 'PRENTICE Alderman of London, the Idle one brought before him & Impeach'd by his Accomplice.

Psalm IX. Ver: 16.)
The Wicked is snar'd in the
work of his own hands

Leviticus CH:XIX.Ve:15.
Thou shall do no unrighteous
ness in Judgment:

Designd & Engraved by Wm Hogarth.

Plate 10.

Publish'd according to Act of Parliament Sepr 30. 1747

138   *Industry and Idleness*, 10: 'The Industrious 'Prentice Alderman of London,
the Idle one brought before him & Impeach'd by his Accomplice', engraving, 1747

accurately represented by the type of broadside sold by the hawker who has   1
a central position in the final scene at Tyburn. That paper, entitled 'The last
dying Speech and Confession of Tho. Idle', would have followed the
familiar form of such penitential writings, in which criminals made last-
minute confessions in order to warn youth against following their example.
Although Hogarth banishes traditional allegory from the scenes themselves their emblematic quality is strengthened by the printed frames which
include, on left or right, emblems of the respective fates of the apprentices:
sceptre and mayoral chain on one side, and manacles, whip and rope on the
other. The quotations from the Scriptures beneath also make a connection
with another popular art form, the sermon.

The engravings are thus in a way both broadsides and sermons, and the

175

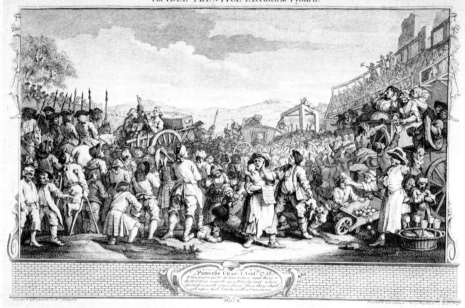

The IDLE 'PRENTICE Executed at Tyburn.

Proverb Chap. I. Vers. 27, 28.

139 *Industry and Idleness*, 11: 'The Idle 'Prentice Executed at Tyburn', engraving, 1747 (see also ill. 1)

134   implied element of sound also contributes to their alienation from the art of the polite world. The orderly rhythm of Goodchild's loom contrasts with Idle's disorderly snoring and the cat's scratching; the harmonious music of a church service with the fall of dice, and so on. These are the sounds of daily life, and in every scene they are suggested – always discordant and eruptive for the Idle Apprentice and harmonious and united for the industrious one. Paulson has also pointed to the way in which the composition of each plate contains contrasts, enclosed and orderly for Goodchild and disorderly for Idle. In gesture, physiognomy and bearing the two are at opposite poles. Yet simple and readable though this language is, ironically it is nearer to the language of Hogarth's History paintings than to that of the Modern Moral

87, 89   Subjects. *Paul before Felix* and *Moses brought to Pharaoh's Daughter* are also works of great readability, for as he claimed of them 'the characters and Expressions were well preserved'.

The *Industry and Idleness* pictures, for all their schematic clarity, are not

176

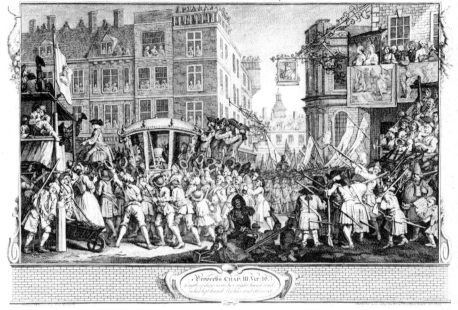

Proverbs CHAP: III. Ver. 16.
*Length of days is in her right hand and
in her left hand Riches and Honour.*

140   *Industry and Idleness*, 12: 'The Industrious 'Prentice Lord-Mayor of London',
engraving, 1747

without humour and satirical touches; indeed it has been argued by Paulson that they contain a kind of counter-argument, an ironical undertone which runs counter to the ostensible moral superiority of industry over idleness. One cannot deny that Goodchild appears as a colourless prig who takes the route of easy advancement, and that each of the plates which feature him contains incidents which recall the untidy morality of the real world. The sixth plate, in which Goodchild, now just married and a partner, offers charity to the musicians, shows them squabbling among themselves, and there is also a hideous legless beggar offering the couple a song. Now it is possible that Hogarth is here including a deliberate irony in order to appeal to the more sophisticated viewer, over the heads, as it were, of the apprentices to which the series was directed. On the other hand, he may simply be trying to show the temptations which stand everywhere in the way of true virtue in this naughty world; it must ever be lonely to be truly virtuous. The issue must rest in the last resort upon one's assessment of Hogarth's

132

177

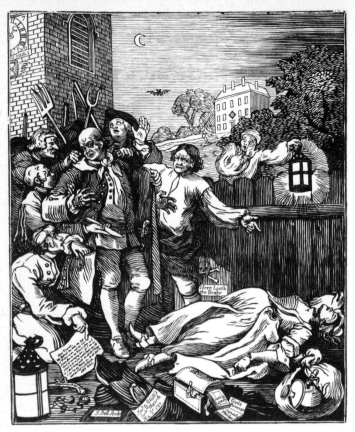

141 *The Four Stages of Cruelty*: 'Cruelty in Perfection', woodcut after Hogarth by John Bell, 1751

character – whether he exhibits at all times the high irony and self-consciousness of Fielding in *Tom Jones*, or, to my mind more likely, that in this case he followed the petit-bourgeois moral earnestness of Samuel Richardson and Lillo, believing that cleverness and wit must give way on occasions to social usefulness.

141–144   The next popular prints, *Beer Street*, *Gin Lane*, and *The Four Stages of Cruelty* of 1751, show Hogarth still more earnestly attempting to achieve more direct images. In announcing them he claimed that 'the Subjects of those Prints are calculated to reform some reigning Vices peculiar to the lower Class of People. In hopes to render them of more extensive Use, the Author has published them in the cheapest Manner possible.' The simplification of effect is taken further, and cheap editions of each print were produced on thin paper. Hogarth even attempted a further reduction by
141   employing a woodcutter, John Bell, to make cheap woodcut versions of the *Four Stages*, but only two were produced before the scheme was abandoned.

178

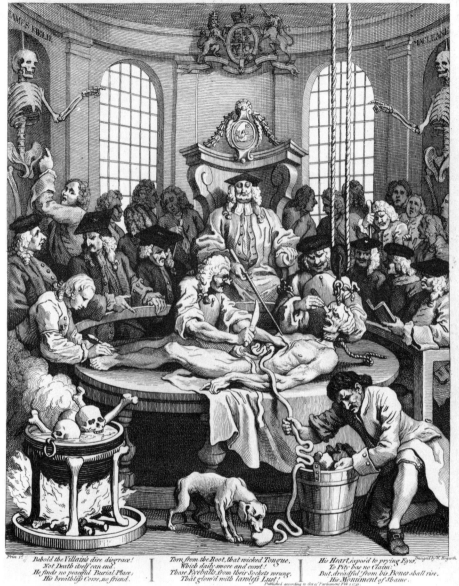

Print 1st.
Behold the Villain's dire disgrace!
Not Death itself can end :
He finds no peaceful Burial-Place ;
His breathless Corse, no friend .

Torn from the Root, that wicked Tongue,
Which daily swore and curst !
Those Eyeballs from their Sockets wrung,
That glow'd with lawless Lust !

His Heart, expos'd to prying Eyes,
To Pity has no Claim :
But, dreadful ! from his Bones shall rise,
His Monument of Shame .

Designed by W. Hogarth.

Published according to Act of Parliament Feb 1.1751

142   *The Four Stages of Cruelty:* 'The Reward of Cruelty', engraving, 1751

143, 144   The 'reigning vices' behind *Beer Street* and *Gin Lane* were, of course, associated with gin drinking, and the publication of the prints was addressed to a specific measure, the passing of the Gin Act of 1751, with heavy punitive measures against distillation – an Act also supported by Fielding, now a magistrate, who may have urged Hogarth to use his talents in a specific campaign. The *Four Stages of Cruelty* were also in sympathy with Fielding's reaction to the horrors of London crime, which he had observed as a magistrate at Bow Street Court in Covent Garden. Tom Nero, the protagonist, descends inexorably from tormenting animals to murdering a

141   maidservant whom he has seduced into stealing her mistress's plate, and
142   equally inexorable is his horrible end in the dissecting room of the Barber-Surgeons' Company. He is shown in the final plate being disembowelled and having his eyes cut out, and the suggestion that he still feels the pain of the knife may refer to the commonest fears of the criminal – that he might not be completely dead from the gibbet and would be snatched away by the surgeons and not buried in peace.

143   *Beer Street* is a representation of an ideal polity, an England in which all foreign elements are rigorously excluded; in the first state of the engraving a scrawny Frenchman is being thrown out by the jolly pipe-smoking black-smith. (Later the blacksmith is holding a leg of beef.) Beer is seen as the drink of good-humour and manly strength, conducive to English robust cheerfulness, in contrast to destructive gin and enervating water, which the writer of the verse under the print urges should be left to France. Beer is the reward for honest labour, serving to celebrate the completion of the building in the background. The newspaper on the table connects this ideal street with the larger polity of England by showing a speech by the King to Parliament in which he earnestly recommends 'the Advancement of Our Commerce, and cultivating the Arts of Peace, in which you may depend on My hearty Concurrence and Encouragement'. In this ideal world the one who suffers is the pawnbroker, who takes advantage of the misery of others and trades behind closed doors. One puzzle is the ragged and scrawny figure of a painter, who is copying a real bottle to make a conventional inn-sign.

144   *Gin Lane* is, of course, the opposite side of the coin and it would be tedious to enumerate the contrasts. Robust good-health gives way to emaciation and death; buildings and structures are now unstable through neglect, and the pawnbroker is king. The ancestry of these prints in Bruegel has often been noted, and they present a kind of secular Last Judgment in which the sinful are in a state of damnation in one and Elysium in the other. Hogarth's Hell is, however, precisely located: it is the notorious parish of St Giles, within sight of St George's, Bloomsbury, Hawksmoor's great church, where

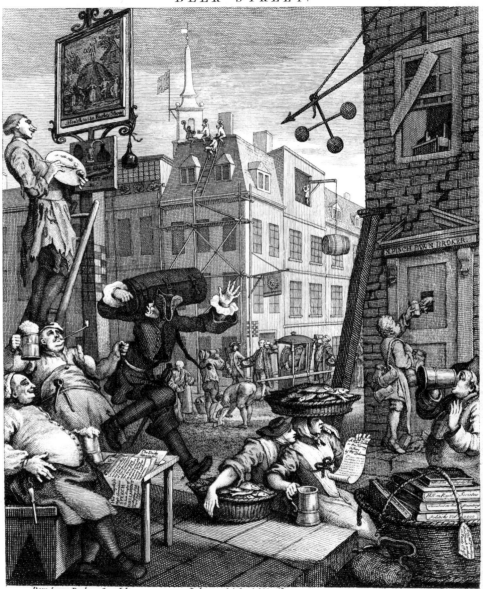

Beer, happy Produce of our Isle
Can sinewy Strength impart.
And wearied with Fatigue and Toil
Can chear each manly Heart.

Labour and Art upheld by Thee
Successfully advance.
We quaff Thy balmy Juice with Glee
And Water leave to France.

Genius of Health, thy grateful Taste
Rivals the Cup of Jove,
And warms each English generous Breast
With Liberty and Love.

143   *Beer Street*, engraving, first state, 1751

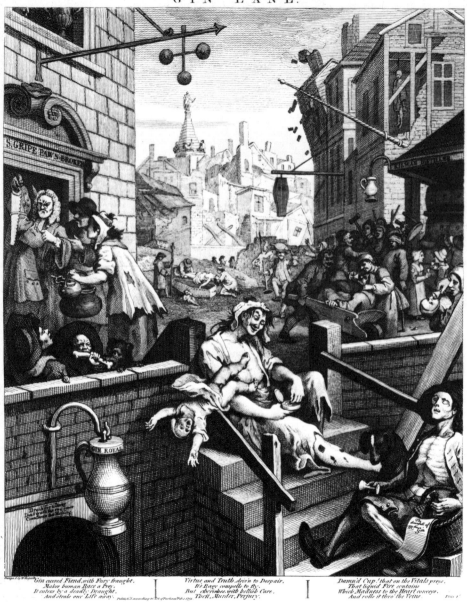

144   *Gin Lane*, engraving, 1751

a statue of George II stands on the extraordinary pyramidal steeple, embodying the harmony of church and civil rule, so wilfully neglected by the inhabitants of Gin Lane.

Hogarth was undoubtedly sincere in believing that his popular prints could lead people away from gin, or prevent 'in some degree that cruel treatment of poor Animals which makes the streets of London more disagreeable to the human mind, than any thing what ever', though to modern ears it seems a rather naive hope. Historians cannot tell us whether anyone was led to constructive virtue by the sight of Hogarth's prints, but we can be sure that his claim was believed by those concerned with social improvement, like schoolmasters and parsons, and his plates were certainly known beyond the circles of the comfortable middle class. Hogarth's strategy of keeping the engraving simple and the prices low was intended to break the piracy whereby a work which was bought by the prosperous would then be copied crudely at a much lower price for the general public. He was determined not to be undercut.

Even at the price of one shilling for each engraving it seems unlikely that many of the really poor could afford *Beer Street* and *Gin Lane*, but we have some glimpses of how Hogarth's prints in general became part of the literal and metaphorical furniture of a wide range of social classes. Dorothy George refers to a pamphlet of 1767, shortly after Hogarth's death, which contains a description of the furnished room of an unmarried clerk in a public office with a salary which would only allow him to live in one of the meaner parts of town like Grub Street itself; despite his poverty, he had on his wall 'two large prints cut in wood and coloured, framed with deal but not glazed, viz. 1.Hogarth's Gate of Calais. 2.Queen Esther and Ahasuerus'. There are also eighteenth-century accounts of schoolmasters using *Industry and Idleness* for moral instruction in the classroom, and we need not doubt that Hogarth's popular prints were disseminated more widely in society than the work of any other 'serious' artist, perhaps in the whole history of art.

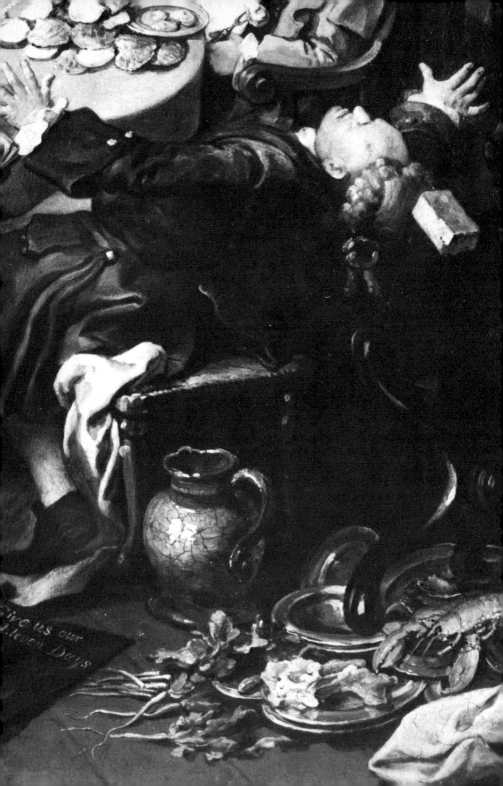

CHAPTER TEN

Bathos

ONE CANNOT CONTEMPLATE HOGARTH'S last years without sadness. By the time he died in 1764 the intellectual world of London was largely alien to him, and while he still had enthusiastic patrons his hopes for the native school were largely thwarted. It is true that a recognizable English school was emerging in his last years, but it followed more the prescription of the connoisseurs, looking to Italy and Greece rather than to the robust life of the London streets. Hogarth's response to defeat became ever more hysterical, and some of the people who knew him in his last years began to wonder if he were not mad. Horace Walpole reported a conversation with him to a friend in 1762: 'My dear Mr Hogarth, I must take leave of you, you now grow too wild – and I left him – if I had stayed, there remained nothing but for him to bite me.' Hogarth was particularly nervous because Walpole was in the process of publishing Vertue's Notebooks, and Hogarth was convinced that he was going to publish material damaging to Thornhill and perhaps to himself. Walpole describes him as harking back to Thornhill whose greatness he reasserted, and warning the visitor against traducing his father-in-law's reputation.

By the 1760s, then, Hogarth was extremely prickly, and it is a sign of his reputation that many continued to brave his bear-like disposition, not always with unhappy results. In fact despite his melancholy he continued to paint as well as ever, and we can see in the paintings of the last decade a deepening of perception and a mellow seriousness which, especially in the portraits, reflects a new understanding of Rembrandt. He was also able to retain on occasion an unaffected gaiety and painterly sensuality, increasing his mastery up to the very end.

These contrasting tendencies can be observed most fully in the four pictures which constitute the *Election* series of 1754 (Sir John Soane's Museum). They are painted generally in a high key and the luminous quality is preserved through virtuoso sweeps of white paint applied broadly to define the cuffs and drapes of the figures. The three outdoor scenes have a spaciousness and sense of atmosphere unprecedented in his work, and *The Polling* has a background with a procession crossing a bridge and a church on a hill beyond, which is painted with an arcadian luminescence that recalls Claude Lorrain, or at least Hogarth's contemporary Richard Wilson.

In these late works we are made even more strongly aware of the discrepancy between the beauty of the painting and the sordidness of some of

145–150

148

185

145   Detail of *The Banquet*, from the *Election* series, 1754
(see ill. 147)

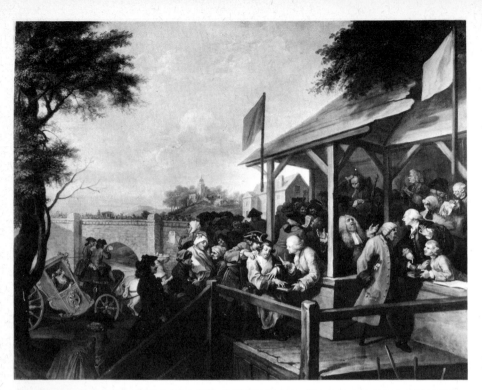

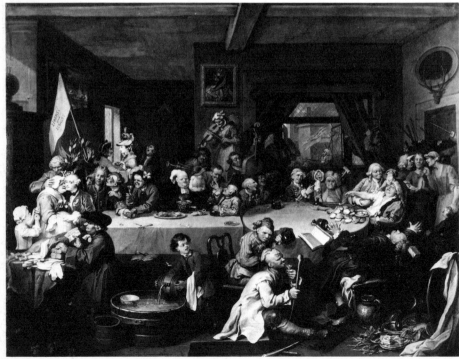

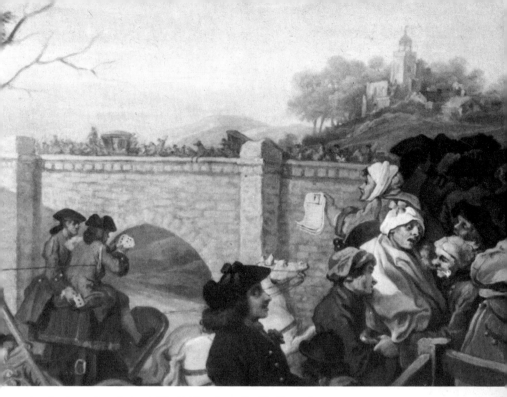

146, 148   *(opposite and above)* *The Polling*, from the *Election* series, 1754

the motifs. In the right-hand corner of *The Banquet* a man hit by a brick is   *145, 147*
seen falling back wounded, but the thick sensual painting of the brick itself
and the Chardinesque still-life of plates laden with food upon which he is
collapsing belie the crude broadsheet quality of the incident. The same may
be said of the group on the opposite side, where the young candidate is
being kissed by a hideous old crone, as a drunk empties his pipe over him
and a child examines his ring covetously. One can find such felicities of
handling throughout the four paintings, yet the underlying themes are
more mordant than ever. There is no redeeming benevolence to be found
anywhere; Hogarth has disdained to provide even one stock figure of
innocence, as he had so often done in the past. One can understand John
Wilkes' complaint that he did not give enough place to benevolence in his
scheme of things. What had once been a Swiftian view of satire hardened in
Hogarth's last years to become a stoical acceptance of the irredeemable
wickedness of the world.

The series depicts a rowdy campaign in the General Election of 1754;
Hogarth has chosen a notoriously corrupt Oxfordshire election as his

187

< 147   *The Banquet*, from the *Election* series, 1754

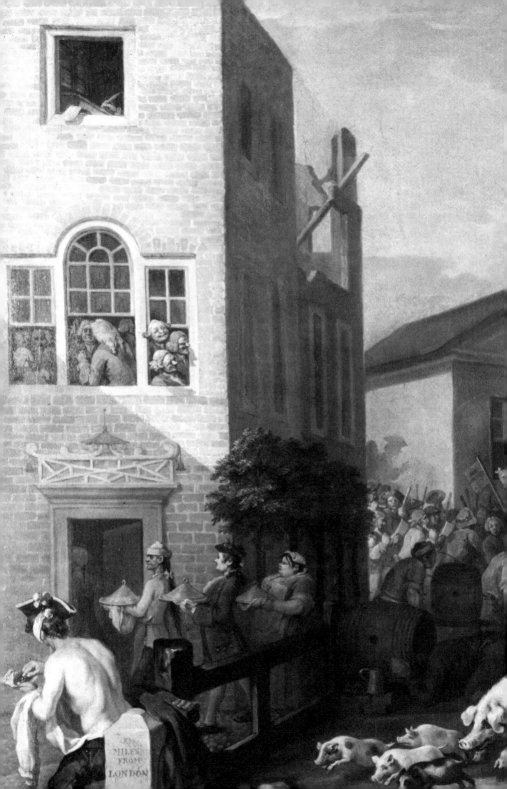

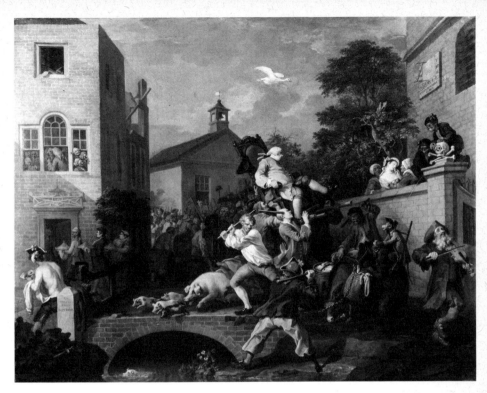

149, 150   *Chairing the Member*, from the *Election* series, 1754

microcosm of the world. There are innumerable topical references in the paintings to such issues as the Jew Bill, which had been the cause of mob hysteria, but these are of secondary importance. Hogarth is not concerned to take the part of either Tory or Whig, though it has been argued that he is implicitly calling for 'a Patriot King' who would, according to Boling-broke's prescription, be above party: rather he is pouring scorn on politi-cians who pander to the mob for short-term advantage, and neglect their true responsibilities. Britannia's coach in *The Polling*, foundering as the drivers cheat at cards, is an obvious allegory of the state of the nation, but in the end the overriding theme is not the corruption of one party, of politi-cians in general, or even the nation in particular, but of the vanity of man-kind. *Chairing the Member* shows that the triumphant politician himself is destined not to enjoy what he has striven for: his triumphal chair is toppled by the efforts of the Gadarene swine who rush underneath to destruction, and he faces his own mortality represented by a skull and crossbones given a pair of eyeglasses by a mischievous chimney sweep.

146

149, 150

189

Despite his crustiness Hogarth was treated with veneration by some, and he occasionally received notable commissions, even one for an immense altarpiece, for the great church of St Mary Redcliffe in Bristol. Objectively speaking Hogarth did not suffer real neglect, but he was haunted by an obsessive feeling of isolation combined with a fear of and hatred for his own times; as with Delacroix in the next century his isolation was more mental than real, but nonetheless erupted frequently into anger and despair. Despite its provincial origin, the St Mary Redcliffe commission was the recognition of his prowess as a History painter that he had long sought, and there were hardly any other artists of the time who could command the fee of £525 that he received for it. The St Mary Redcliffe Altarpiece (which now belongs to Bristol City Art Gallery) has rarely attracted favourable comment, and most recently Paulson censured the paintings as 'the effort of a tired, aging, and perhaps ailing man'. They are admittedly rather old-fashioned in their treatment, and the triptych format clearly presented great difficulties, for in the original position the wings could only be viewed at a sharp angle – something which in fact perfectly explains their curious composition with spread-out figures. The central panel of the *Ascension* owes something of its compositional structure to Raphael's *Transfiguration*, which it follows in the disorderly grouping of the human activities compared with the radiant harmony of Christ's ascent. Seen from the far end of the nave of St Mary Redcliffe (whence the altarpiece was removed in the 1850s), the division

151   St Mary Redcliffe, Bristol, with Hogarth's altarpiece in its original position (drawing by James Johnson, 1828)

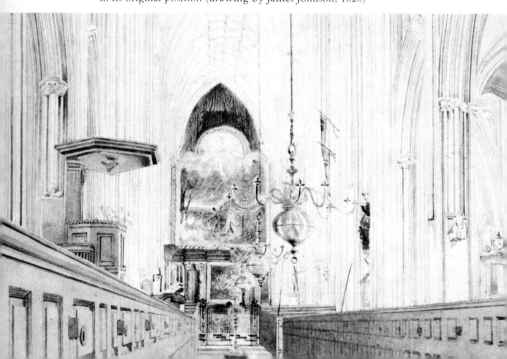

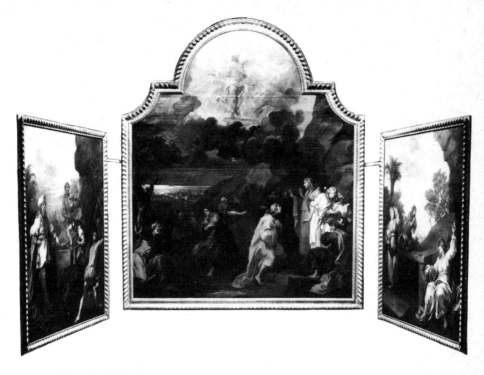

152   St Mary Redcliffe Altarpiece, 1755–56

between the earthly and heavenly realms must have taken on extra force from the soaring verticality of the setting, giving the worshipper the sense of belonging with the worldly hubbub of the disciples and yet aspiring to the glory above. Hogarth was instinctively more in sympathy with the architecture than he is usually given credit for, and the almost overwhelming substantiality of all the figures except Christ is not without a theological point. It is true that some of the figures are somewhat leaden and there is something comic in the voluminousness of their draperies (apart from the intentional comedy of the High Priest having the tomb sealed apparently with wax), but the colour and light which radiates from the ascending Saviour is of incomparable beauty, and there are extraordinary felicities like the flash of lightning which illuminates the Holy City beyond. The altarpiece is a work of outstanding presence, and although many English religious paintings of the eighteenth century have a more harmonious structure, none surpasses it in expression and power of conception.

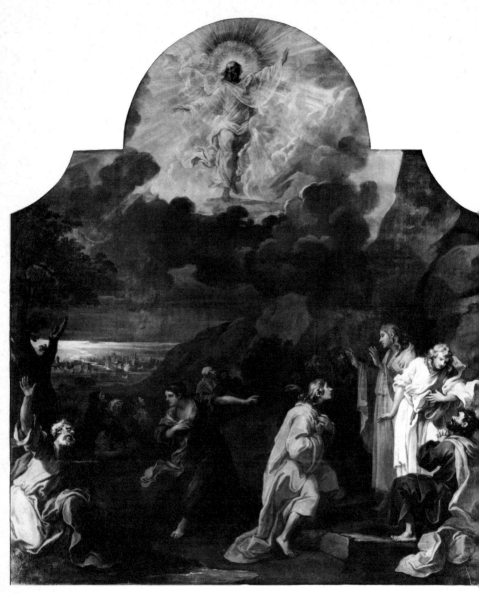

153   *The Ascension*, central panel of the St Mary Redcliffe Altarpiece, 1755–56

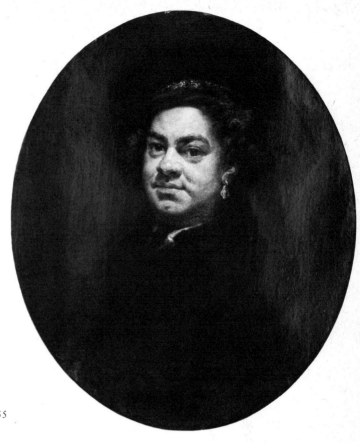

154   *John Pine, c.* 1755

In 1757 Hogarth made the surprising announcement in the press that he intended 'to employ the rest of his Time in PORTRAIT PAINTING chiefly'. Clearly he did not expect to become at this stage a fashionable portraitist, and it is possible that the gesture sprang from weariness, for he had never regarded portrait painting as a very arduous enterprise. He apparently offered as an innovation the claim that he could make a complete portrait from four fifteen-minute sittings. Despite this characteristic bravado his last portraits have nothing of the summariness that one might expect. Indeed they are more than anything Rembrandtesque, and the painting of his friend the engraver John Pine (Beaverbrook Art Gallery, Fredericton) is a *154* conscious imitation of a late self-portrait by the Dutch master. The influence of Rembrandt on the last portraits should not, however, be seen as

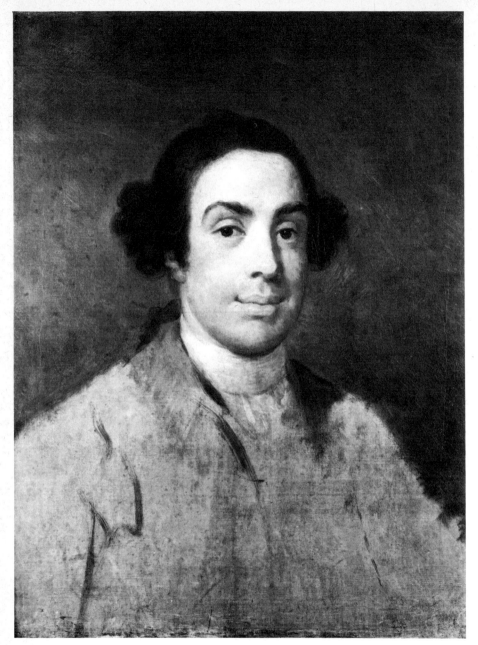

155　*James Caulfield, 1st Earl of Charlemont, c. 1759*

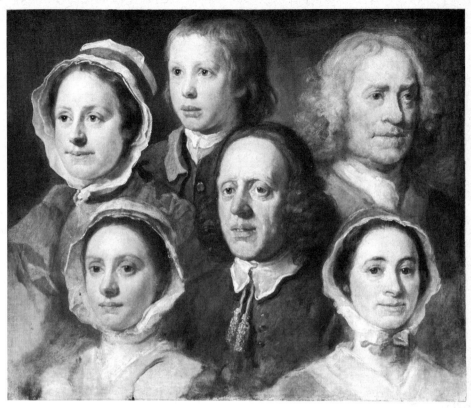

156   *Heads of Six of Hogarth's Servants, c.* 1750–55

'imitation' in the eighteenth-century sense, like painting the sitter in Van
Dyck costume: it is reflected more in a deeper sense of humanity achieved
by a more emphatic chiaroscuro. The inheritance from Rembrandt through
Kneller had now been transformed into an intimation of a richer humanity
transcending social class. This can be found in such unfinished paintings as
The 1st Earl of Charlemont (Smith College Museum of Art, Northampton,   *155*
Mass.), and most movingly of all in the group of heads of his servants (Tate   *156*
Gallery). There is no hint of satire here, or in any of the last portraits.

    Nor is there any satire in Hogarth's last self-portrait, *The Artist painting*   *158*
the Comic Muse of 1758 (National Portrait Gallery); the engaging irony and
bluff directness of the *Self-Portrait* of 1745 have completely gone. The artist
shows himself as extremely vulnerable, even diminutive, seated before a
canvas with the bare outline laid in of Thalia, the Muse of Comedy. The

195

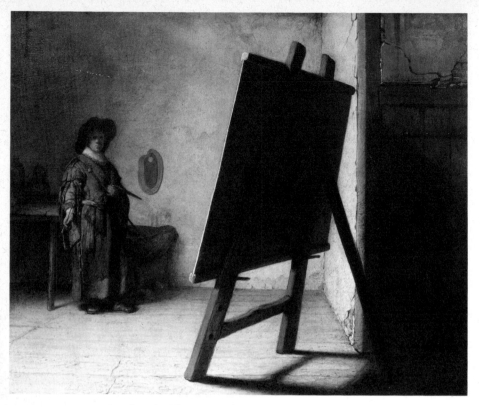

157   Rembrandt: *The Artist in his Studio*, late 1620s

abstractness of the theme is quite at odds with the intimacy and realism of the portrait. The type of the artist painting his muse is not uncommon, but in spirit Hogarth's picture bears comparison not with previous representa-

157   tions of the subject but with the extraordinary early *Self-Portrait* by Rembrandt in the Boston Museum of Fine Arts, which appears to express the humility the artist might feel before his great task. Hogarth, it must be said, did not readily feel humility, and one should see the late *Self-Portrait* more as an expression of valedictory despair.

The polemical nature of the painting brings us back to the writings of Hogarth's last years, to which, as he found painting more tiring, he devoted so much time. The salient themes of those writings have been discussed in an earlier chapter, and *The Apology for Painters*, which he was probably working on when Walpole called on him, like his conversation bears the

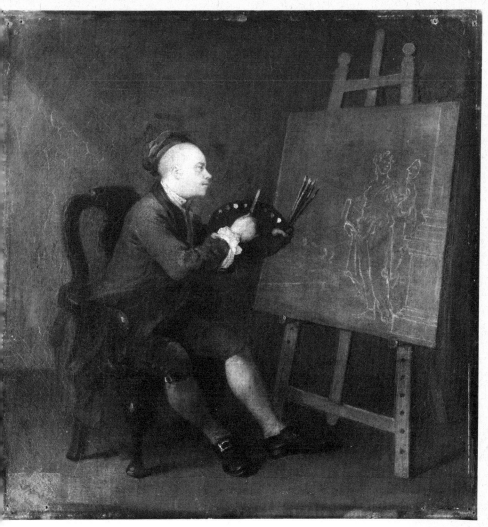

158   *The Artist painting the Comic Muse,* 1758

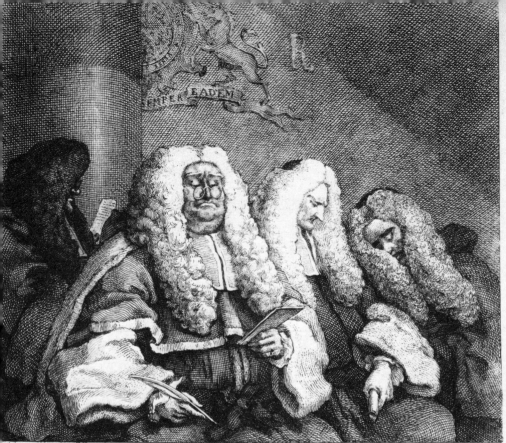

sign'd & Engrav'd by W. Hogarth

The BENCH.

Publish'd as the Act directs 4 Sep. 1758.

 the different meaning of the Words Character, Caracatura and Outrè in Painting and Drawing.
Addrefs'd to the Hon.ble Coll. ....d.

There are hardly any two things more essentially different than Character and Caracatura nevertheless
they are usually confounded and mistaken for each other: on which account this Explanation is attempted.
It has ever been allow'd that, when a Character is strongly markd in the living Face, it may be consider'd as
an Index of the mind, to express which with any degree of justness in Painting, requires the utmost Efforts of a great
Master. Now that which has, of late Years, got the name of Caracatura, is, or ought to be totally divested of every
Stroke that hath a tendancy to good Drawing: it may be said to be a Species of Lines that are produc'd rather by the
hand of chance than of Skill: for the early Scrawlings of a Child which do but barely hint an Idea of an Human
Face, will always be found to be like some Person or other, and will often form such a Comical Resemblance
as in all probability the most eminent Caracaturers of these times will not be able to equal with Design, because their Ideas of Objects are so much more perfect than Childrens, that they will unavoidably introduce some
kind of Drawing: for all the humourous Effects of the fashionable manner of Caracaturing chiefly depend on
the surprize we are under at finding our selves caught with any sort of Similitude in objects absolutely remote in their kind. Let it be observ'd the more remote in their Nature the greater is the Excellence of these
Pieces; as a proof of this, I remember a famous Caracatura of a certain Italian Singer, that Struck at
first sight, which consisted only of a Streight perpendicular Stroke with a Dot over it. As to the French
word Outrè it is different from the foregoing, and signifies nothing more than the exagerated
outlines of a Figure, all the parts of which may be in other respects a perfect and true Picture of
Nature. A Giant may be call'd a common Man Outrè. So any part as a Nose, or a Leg, made
igger than it ought to be, is that part Outrè, † which is all that is to be understood by this word, so
injudiciously us'd to the prejudice of Character. ——

† See Excess Analysis of Beauty, Chap. 6.

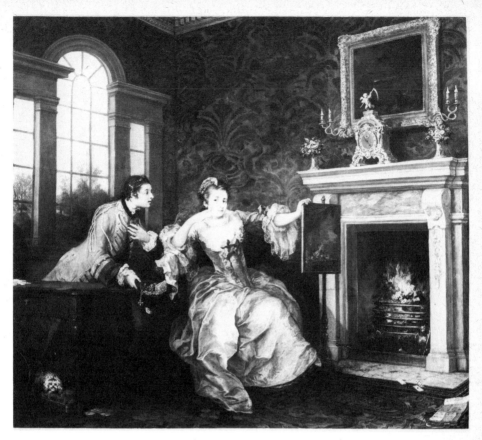

160   *The Lady's Last Stake*, 1759

marks of dangerous obsession. He could not resist making further demonstrations of his ideas, and using his paintings and engravings for what he
termed 'ocular demonstrations'. The tiny painting called *The Bench*, of 1758
(Fitzwilliam Museum, Cambridge), which shows a fat and pompous judge
presiding over his sleeping colleagues, was engraved with a long inscription   *159*
in which the distinction between character and caricature is reiterated, and
which Hogarth was apparently still correcting on his deathbed.

Even a commission to make a risqué painting, *The Lady's Last Stake*, for   *160*
an aristocratic collector became an occasion for a rehearsal of his theories
about the taste for Old Master paintings. This well-documented episode is
especially revealing for it highlights with great clarity his ambivalent
attitude towards his own art which grew more pronounced at the end.

199

< 159   *The Bench*, engraving, 1758

Hogarth had been prevailed upon by Lord Charlemont to paint one more 'Comic History': 'The subject was a virtuous married lady that had lost all at cards to a young officer, wavering at his suit whether she should part with her Honour or no to regain the loss.' The painting (Albright-Knox Art Gallery, Buffalo), despite all of Hogarth's protestations of tiredness, is a tour-de-force in the high-life manner of *Marriage-a-la-Mode*, and perhaps even surpasses it in painterly quality and wit. Despite the air of erotic dalliance, there is a touching eagerness in the officer's importunity which
32, 37 recalls the earlier *Before* and *After* paintings.

Not surprisingly the patron was delighted and showed it to his friends, one of whom, Sir Richard Grosvenor, being as Hogarth tells us 'infinitely rich pressed me with more vehemence to do what subject I would upon the same terms much against my inclination'. Hogarth with characteristic
161 perversity chose a tragic subject from history rather than a comic subject from contemporary life, no doubt with the intention of providing a pendant to the other picture which would show the range of his talent and capabilities. The choice of the subject was guided by the high price paid for a painting falsely attributed to Correggio (in fact by the seventeenth-century Florentine Francesco Furini) of the gory subject from Boccaccio of Sigismonda contemplating the heart of her beloved, a family retainer who had been brutally murdered by her father. Sir Richard Grosvenor was quite dismayed and refused the picture, which was universally ridiculed, and it remained so notorious that a later owner hired it out as an example of how *not* to paint in the Grand Manner. The subject is undoubtedly melodramatic, and Hogarth has unashamedly modelled it on the stage, claiming that 'people's hearts were as touched as I have seen them at a Tragedy'. Although we still find more enjoyment in the depiction of aristocratic dalliance than of the noble love of past ages, we must grant that *Sigismonda* is painted with wonderful breadth and richness.

The catastrophe of *Sigismonda* came in 1759 and was one of the many misfortunes which beset Hogarth's last years, as he himself noted: 'The anxiety which attended this affair and the recollection of ideas long dormant, coming at a time when nature rather wants a quieter life and something to cheer it, brought on an illness which continued for a year.' Yet one should not imagine that Hogarth spent his final years in lonely isolation; the howl of pain which emerges from his late writings did not entirely drown his clubbable spirit. Aside from his oft-recorded presence in coffee-houses and men's clubs like the Beefsteak he was also something of a committee man. He kept the St Martin's Lane Academy going through the 1740s and early 50s, and he became in 1755 an early member of the Society for the Encouragement of the Arts, Manufactures and Commerce, an organization intended

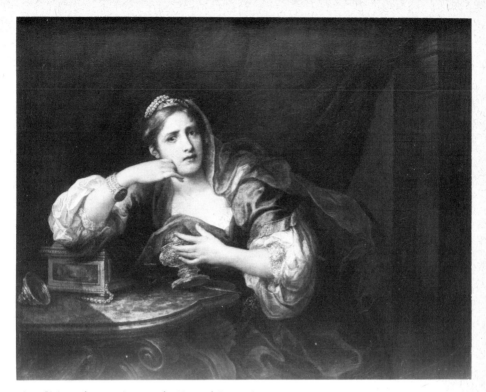

161   *Sigismonda mourning over the Heart of Guiscardo*, 1759

to improve standards of industrial design and invention, which still flourishes today. He soon quarrelled with them and left, but he remained concerned with the problem of exhibiting the works of young artists, and was an active member of the Society of Artists, one of the many groups seeking to promote a national academy of art.

The foundation of the Society of Artists in 1759 was a turning point in the campaign for what was to be the Royal Academy of Arts, and the movement was to gain momentum with the advent of a new king, George III, in 1760. Hogarth's fear expressed in his *Apology for Painters* was that the Academy would turn out to be on the rigidly hierarchical French model, no doubt with the subtle and ambitious Reynolds as President, instead of the freer and more open system of his and Thornhill's academy. Hogarth fought vigorously against the notion of a formal academy, causing a secession in the Society of Artists and gathering around him a group of anti-connoisseurs including the great sculptor Roubiliac.

165

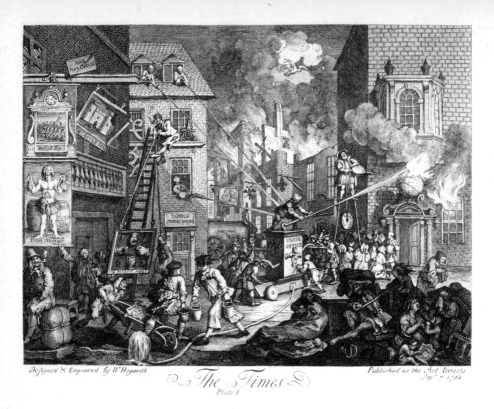

162   *The Times, Plate I*, engraving, 1762

Hogarth like every public figure of the time was frequently attacked in the press and through caricatures, but the attacks were rarely malicious, and he could comfort himself with the support of a large number of friends and admirers. Late in 1762 he suddenly found himself the butt of real savagery, which he had to some degree unleashed himself. In the 1750s Hogarth appears to have been clarifying his political allegiance and moving steadily towards the Court interest. There are hints that he saw the best hope for the arts not in the merchant class but in an enlightened monarchy, and he made efforts to attach himself to the party of the future George III; by becoming Serjeant-Painter to the King in 1757, in belated succession to Thornhill, he had become in effect a placeman. This shift was not perhaps so dramatic as is often thought, for despite his instinctive sympathy with many of its attitudes his allegiance to the mercantile class was always tenuous. After producing a bizarre attack on Methodism and the Church in Spring 1762, in the print *Credulity, Superstition and Fanaticism*, he then, perhaps encouraged by his political friends, produced a political print, and an unashamedly

partisan one. *The Times, Plate I* proclaims the Earl of Bute as a lone fire- 162
fighter trying to put out the flames of war fanned for the sake of profit by
Pitt and the mercantile interest, who are mercilessly lampooned.

Unluckily for Hogarth many of his friends, like John Wilkes and Charles
Churchill, the editor of *The North Briton*, were hostile to peace, and aside
from their immediate political grievances they felt Hogarth to be a worthy
opponent. Churchill wrote, 'there is no credit to be got by breaking flies
upon a wheel. But Hogarths are Subjects worthy of an Englishman's pen.'
Hogarth was apparently warned in advance by Wilkes that he would
retaliate if attacked, and friends of Hogarth, like Garrick, who were aware
of the dangers of offending such a formidable polemicist as Wilkes, tried to
stave off the inevitable attack in *The North Briton*. In the event it came swiftly
and was all the more damaging for recognizing Hogarth's gifts and adopt-
ing a tone of weary regret at the downfall of such a talent. The nub of the
attack was that Hogarth in his dotage had given up what Wilkes calls 'the
rare talents of gibbeting in colours' to attempt sublime History which was
beyond his powers (as evinced by *Sigismonda*), and he had descended to
factional politics and personal abuse. There was a grain of truth in the
accusation, as Hogarth and all his contemporaries well knew, and to make
things worse it came at a time of illness; as Hogarth pathetically recorded,
'it could not but hurt a feeling mind'.

Even Wilkes believed that his article had administered a death-blow to
Hogarth, but in fact the artist did begin work on a sequel, *The Times,
Plate 2*, which he did not live to complete, and he was also able to hit back at
Wilkes effectively. Wilkes was arrested after an attack on the King in the
famous Number 45 of *The North Briton*, and Hogarth by his own account
went to the court to draw him and produce a portrait 'done as like as I
could to feature, at the same time some indication of his mind fully answerd
my purpose'. The result was a devastating caricature which achieves its 163
effects by a relatively slight distortion of Wilkes's features (which did
include a squint), to suggest the leering rake beneath the protestations of
principle. If the satirist's victory lies with posterity then Hogarth won this
contest, but it was a Pyrrhic victory. Hogarth then had to take on his next
opponent, Charles Churchill, an equally formidable adversary, who, perhaps to increase Hogarth's anxiety, held his fire for a while. When it arrived
it was something of a damp squib, and Hogarth was no doubt relieved that
it contained no new accusations or home truths. Hogarth's reply was to
burnish out his own image from the *Self-Portrait with Pug* engraving and 119
replace it with a drunken bear representing Churchill. The tremendous 164
cause celèbre, which was much discussed in the press and coffee-houses,
fizzled out like a match between two elderly prizefighters.

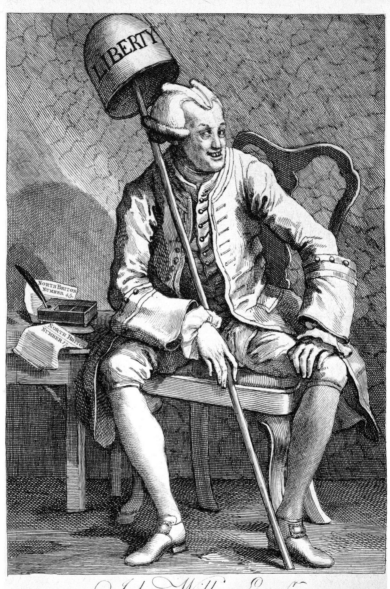

163 *John Wilkes*, etching, 1763

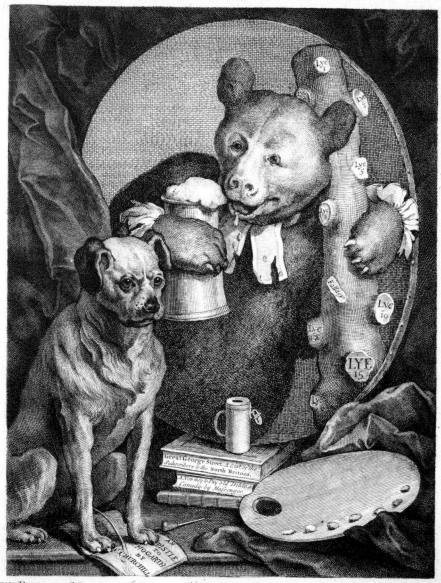

THE BRUISER, C. CHURCHILL (once the Rev.ᵈ) in the Character of a Modern Hercules, Regaling himself after having Kill'd the Monster Caricatura that so sorely Gall'd his Virtuous friend the Heaven born WILKES.

— But he had a Club this Dragon to Drub,   Or he had ne'er don't I warrant ye.—

Designd and Engraved by Wᵐ Hogarth Price 1ˢ

Published according to Act of Parliament August 1. 1763.

164   'The Bruiser, C. Churchill', engraving, 1763

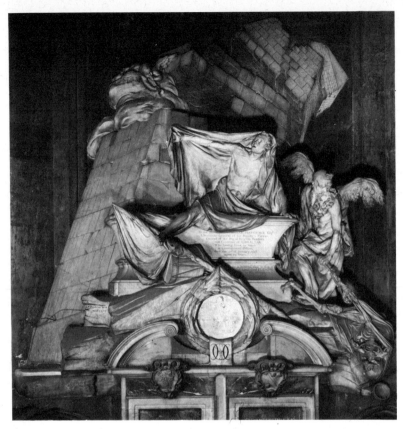

165   Louis François Roubiliac: monument of General Hargrave, 1757

Despite persistent rumours, Hogarth was not driven to his deathbed by
these public squabbles, but he was not in good health and no doubt he felt
his end to be near. His occupations at the end were to work on his autobiography, rework some of his plates, and create one final engraving. The
last autobiographical writings are hardly bearable to read: he returns
obsessively to the prejudices of the connoisseurs and hammers home his
166   ideas with shrill repetitiveness. The ostensible purpose of his print, *The
Bathos*, was to act as a tailpiece to the collected volume of his engravings,
but it was also valedictory. It is a work of unmitigated pessimism, employing symbols associated with funerary monuments but with no hint of
redemption, inverting such imagery as that used by Roubiliac for the
165   Hargrave tomb completed in 1757 in Westminster Abbey, London, where

the weariness of Time is contrasted with the hope of resurrection, as the Last Trump is blown. In Hogarth everything is on the point of dissolution: the sun is going out, the church is in ruins, nature is bankrupt; only a tombstone with a grinning deathshead remains permanent. And Hogarth himself is going out, for among the detritus surrounding Father Time there is a copy of his *The Times* engraving catching fire, and a broken palette; the end of his life is the end of the world. The print was published at the beginning of March 1764, and he lingered on, writing more of his autobiography and tinkering with old plates, until October, when he died.

166   *The Bathos*, engraving, 1764

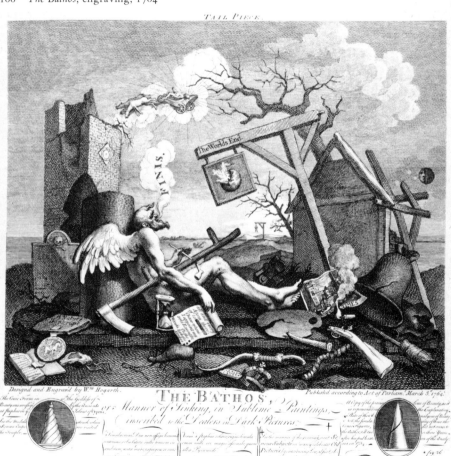

Bibliography

THE MOST COMPREHENSIVE and recent biography of Hogarth is Ronald Paulson, *Hogarth: His Life, Art, and Times* (New Haven and London, 1971). Of Hogarth's own writings, *The Analysis of Beauty* was edited by Joseph Burke (Oxford, 1955), in a volume which includes the *Autobiographical Notes*, and *An Apology for Painters* was edited by Michael Kitson for the Walpole Society (XLI, 1966–68).

The most recent catalogue of the paintings is R. B. Beckett, *Hogarth* (London, 1949); for the drawings see A. P. Oppé, *The Drawings of William Hogarth* (London, 1948); and for the prints Ronald Paulson, *Hogarth's Graphic Works* (New Haven and London, 1965, abridged ed. 1970).

For more general reading and ideas I would recommend F. Antal, *Hogarth and his Place in European Art* (London, 1962), and Lawrence Gowing's catalogue of the Tate Gallery exhibition (London, 1971). There have also been innumerable worthwhile articles on aspects of Hogarth in the *Journal of the Warburg and Courtauld Institutes* and *The Burlington Magazine*.

There are many books on the period which only mention Hogarth in passing, but are extremely useful for understanding him. The ones I have found most helpful are: Pat Rogers, *Grub Street* (London, 1972) and *The Augustan Vision* (London and New York, 1974); M. D. George, *London Life in the Eighteenth Century* (London and New York, 1925; Harmondsworth and Baltimore, 1966); and D. Hay *et al.*, *Albion's Fatal Tree* (Harmondsworth and Baltimore, 1975).

List of Illustrations

Measurements are given in inches and centimetres, height before width

28 *The Woodes Rogers Family*, 1729. Oil on canvas, 14 × 18 (35.6 × 45.7). The National Maritime Museum, London

29 *The Cholmondeley Family*, 1732. Oil on canvas, 28 × $35\frac{3}{4}$ (71 × 76.2). Private Collection. Photo The Paul Mellon Centre for Studies in British Art

30, 31 *The House of Cards*, I and II, 1730. Oil on canvas, each 25 × 30 (63.5 × 76). Private Collection. Photo The Paul Mellon Centre for Studies in British Art

32 *Before*, 1730–31. Oil on canvas, $15\frac{1}{4}$ × $13\frac{1}{4}$ (38.7 × 33.6). The J. Paul Getty Museum, Malibu, California

33 *After*, 1730–31. Oil on canvas, $15\frac{1}{4}$ × $13\frac{1}{4}$ (38.7 × 33.6). The J. Paul Getty Museum, Malibu, California

34 FRANÇOIS DE TROY (attr.) *Louis XIV and his Heirs*, *c.* 1709. Oil on canvas, $50\frac{7}{8}$ × $63\frac{7}{8}$ (129.2 × 162.2). Reproduced by permission of the Trustees of the Wallace Collection, London

35 PHILIPPE MERCIER *A Hanoverian Party on a Terrace, with the Schutz Family, cousins of George II*, 1725. Oil on canvas, $40\frac{1}{4}$ × $49\frac{1}{2}$ (102 × 125.7). The Tate Gallery, London

36 *Ashley Cowper with his Wife and Daughter*, 1731. Oil on canvas, 21 × $23\frac{7}{8}$ (53.3 × 60.6). The Tate Gallery, London

37 *Before*, 1730–31. Oil on canvas, $14\frac{5}{8}$ × $17\frac{5}{8}$ (37 × 44.8). Reproduced by permission of the Syndics of the Fitzwilliam Museum, Cambridge

38 *After*, 1730–31. Oil on canvas, $14\frac{5}{8}$ × $17\frac{3}{4}$ (37 × 45). Reproduced by permission of the Syndics of the Fitzwilliam Museum, Cambridge

39 *A Prisoner of the Fleet being examined*, 1729. Oil on paper, $18\frac{1}{2}$ × $23\frac{1}{2}$ (47 × 60). Reproduced by permission of the Syndics of the Fitzwilliam Museum, Cambridge

40 *The Committee of the House of Commons on the Fleet Prison*, 1729. Oil on canvas, 20 × 27 (50.8 × 68.6). National Portrait Gallery, London

41 *John Huggins*, before 1745. Oil on canvas, 18 × $15\frac{3}{4}$ (45.7 × 40). The Hyde Collection, Somerville, New Jersey. Photo The Paul Mellon Centre for Studies in British Art

42 *A Harlot's Progress*, 1, 1731. Engraving, $11\frac{3}{4}$ × $14\frac{3}{4}$ (29.8 × 37.5)

43 *A Harlot's Progress*, 2, 1731. Engraving, $11\frac{7}{8}$ × $14\frac{5}{8}$ (30 × 37.8)

44 *A Harlot's Progress*, 3, 1731. Engraving, $11\frac{3}{4}$ × $14\frac{3}{4}$ (29.8 × 37.5)

45 *A Harlot's Progress*, 4, 1731. Engraving, $11\frac{3}{4}$ × $14\frac{3}{4}$ (29.8 × 37.5)

46 *A Harlot's Progress*, 5, 1731. Engraving, 12 × $14\frac{3}{4}$ (30.5 × 37.5)

47 *A Harlot's Progress*, 6, 1731. Engraving, $11\frac{3}{4}$ × $14\frac{3}{4}$ (29.8 × 37.5)

48 *The Marriage Contract*, *c.* 1732. Oil on canvas, $24\frac{3}{4}$ × $29\frac{1}{2}$ (62 × 75). Reproduced by permission of the Visitors of the Ashmolean Museum, Oxford

49–56 *The Rake's Progress*, 1–8, 1733–34. Oil on canvas, each $24\frac{1}{2}$ × $29\frac{1}{2}$ (62.2 × 75). By courtesy of the Trustees of Sir John Soane's Museum, London

57 Detail of *Morning*, 1738. Oil on canvas, 29 × 24 (73.7 × 61). The National Trust (Bearsted Collection, Upton House, Warwickshire)

58 Map of London, Westminster and Southwark, by Thomas Bowles, 1744. Engraving

59 Hanover Square, London. Engraving by Sutton Nicholls

60 View from the window of the merchant's house, detail of the last scene of *Marriage-a-la-Mode*: see ill. 84. Reproduced by courtesy of the Trustees of the National Gallery, London

61 Looking from Piccadilly to St James's Palace, detail of scene 4 of *The Rake's Progress*: see ills. 49–56. By courtesy of the Trustees of Sir John Soane's Museum, London

62 Detail of *Southwark Fair*: see ill. 64

63 FRANCIS HAYMAN *The See-Saw*, *c.* 1740–43. Oil on canvas, $53\frac{3}{4}$ × 95 (136.5 × 241). The Tate Gallery, London

64 *Southwark Fair*, 1733. Engraving, $13\frac{1}{2}$ × $17\frac{7}{8}$ (34.3 × 45.4)

65 *Morning*, 1738. Engraving, $18\frac{1}{8}$ × $14\frac{7}{8}$ (46 × 37.8)

66 *Noon*, 1738. Oil on canvas, $29\frac{1}{2}$ × $24\frac{1}{2}$ (75 × 62). Private Collection

67 *Evening*, 1738. Oil on canvas, $29\frac{1}{2}$ × $24\frac{1}{2}$ (75 × 62). Private Collection

68 *Night*, 1738. Engraving, $17\frac{5}{8}$ × $14\frac{1}{2}$ (44.8 × 36.8)

69, 70 *Strolling Actresses dressing in a Barn*, 1738. Engraving, $16\frac{3}{4}$ × $21\frac{1}{4}$ (42.5 × 54)

71 JACOPO AMICONI *Mercury about to slay Argus*, 1730–32. Oil on canvas, 25 × $25\frac{1}{4}$ (63.5 × 64). The Tate Gallery, London

72 *Heads from the Raphael Cartoons*, after Thornhill. Engraved early 1730s, published 1781. $8\frac{1}{2}$ × $13\frac{7}{8}$ (21.5 × 35.2). Andrew Edmunds

73 *The Pool of Bethesda*, wall-painting in St Bartholomew's Hospital, London, 1735–37. Oil on canvas. Photo Medical Illustration Department, St Bartholomew's Hospital, London

74 Academy study for *The Pool of Bethesda*, c. 1735–36. Black and white chalk on brown paper, $14\frac{5}{8} \times 11\frac{1}{4}$ (37 × 28.5). Royal Library, Windsor Castle. Reproduced by gracious permission of Her Majesty Queen Elizabeth II

75 Detail of *The Good Samaritan*, wall-painting in St Bartholomew's Hospital, London, 1735–37. Oil on canvas. Photo Medical Illustration Department, St Bartholomew's Hospital, London

76 Musicians and dancing master at the Countess's Levée, detail of scene 4 of *Marriage-a-la-Mode*: see ill. 82. Reproduced by courtesy of the Trustees of the National Gallery, London. Photo Eileen Tweedy

77 'Characters and Caricaturas', subscription ticket for *Marriage-a-la-Mode*, 1743. Engraving, second state, $7\frac{7}{8} \times 8\frac{1}{8}$ (20 × 20.6)

78 HUBERT GRAVELOT *Le Lecteur*, or *The Judicious Lover*. Oil on canvas, $12\frac{1}{4} \times 9\frac{3}{8}$ (31 × 23.8). Marble Hill House, Twickenham (Greater London Council)

79 *Marriage-a-la-Mode*, I: the Marriage Contract, 1743. Oil on canvas, 27 × 35 (68.6 × 89). Reproduced by courtesy of the Trustees of The National Gallery, London

80, 81 *Marriage-a-la-Mode*, II: After the Marriage, 1743. Oil on canvas, 27 × 35 (68.6 × 89). Reproduced by courtesy of the Trustees of the National Gallery, London. Colour photo Eileen Tweedy

82 *Marriage-a-la-Mode*, IV: the Countess's Levée, 1743. Oil on canvas, 27 × 35 (68.6 × 89). Reproduced by courtesy of the Trustees of the National Gallery, London

83, 85 *Marriage-a-la-Mode*, V: the Death of the Earl, 1743. Oil on canvas, whole picture 27 × 35 (68.6 × 89). Reproduced by courtesy of the Trustees of the National Gallery, London. Colour photo Eileen Tweedy

84 *Marriage-a-la-Mode*, VI: the Death of the Countess, 1743. Oil on canvas, 27 × 35 (68.6 × 89). Reproduced by courtesy of the Trustees of the National Gallery, London

86 JOSEPH HIGHMORE *Pamela is Married*, 1743–44. Oil on canvas, $25\frac{1}{2} \times 31\frac{1}{2}$ (64.8 × 80). The Tate Gallery, London

87 *Paul before Felix*, 1748. Oil on canvas, 120 × 168 (304.8 × 426.7). The Honourable Society of Lincoln's Inn, London

88, 89 *Moses brought to Pharaoh's Daughter*, 1746. Oil on canvas, whole picture 63 × 82 (172.7 × 208). The Thomas Coram Foundation for Children, London. Colour photo Eileen Tweedy; black-and-white photo The Paul Mellon Centre for Studies in British Art

90 FRANCIS HAYMAN *The Finding of Moses*, 1746. Oil on canvas, $68\frac{1}{4} \times 80\frac{1}{2}$ (173.4 × 204.5). The Thomas Coram Foundation for Children, London. Photo The Paul Mellon Centre for Studies in British Art

91 Study, possibly connected with a lost painting of *Danaë*. Pencil with chalk highlights on buff paper, $10\frac{1}{4} \times 17\frac{1}{4}$

(26 × 43.4). Yale Center for British Art, Paul Mellon Collection

92 Burlesque of *Paul before Felix*, 1751. Engraving, $9\frac{7}{8} \times 13\frac{1}{2}$ (25 × 34)

93 *William Cavendish, 4th Duke of Devonshire*, 1741. Oil on canvas, $29\frac{7}{8} \times 25$ (76 × 63.5). Yale Center for British Art, Paul Mellon Collection

94 After THOMAS HUDSON *William Cavendish, 4th Duke of Devonshire*. Oil on canvas, $29\frac{1}{2} \times 24\frac{1}{2}$ (75 × 62). The National Trust (Hardwick Hall, Derbyshire)

95 *Thomas Herring, Archbishop of Canterbury*, 1744. Oil on canvas, 50 × 40 (127 × 101.5). The Tate Gallery, London

96 J. B. VANLOO *Richard Temple, 1st Viscount Cobham*, c. 1718. Oil on canvas, $29\frac{5}{8} \times 24\frac{3}{8}$ (75 × 62). Collection Viscount Cobham, Hagley Hall, West Midlands. Photo Courtauld Institute of Art, London

97 *Sir Robert Pye*, 1730. Oil on canvas, $16\frac{7}{8} \times 13\frac{1}{4}$ (43 × 33.6). Marble Hill House, Twickenham (Greater London Council)

98 FRANCIS HAYMAN *John Conyers*, probably 1747. Oil on canvas, $21\frac{1}{4} \times 18\frac{1}{4}$ (54 × 46). Marble Hill House, Twickenham (Greater London Council)

99 *Benjamin Hoadly, Bishop of Winchester*, c. 1738. Oil on canvas, 24 × 29 (61 × 73.5). Henry E. Huntington Library and Art Gallery, San Marino, California

100 *Benjamin Hoadly, Bishop of Winchester*, c. 1743. Oil on canvas, $49\frac{1}{2} \times 39\frac{1}{2}$ (125.7 × 100). The Tate Gallery, London

101 *Captain Thomas Coram*,

1740. Oil on canvas, 94 × 58 (238.7 × 147). The Thomas Coram Foundation for Children, London. Photo The Paul Mellon Centre for Studies in British Art

102 After HYACINTHE RIGAUD *Samuel Bernard*, 1729. Engraving by Pierre Drevet, $24\frac{3}{8}$ × $16\frac{5}{8}$ (61.9 × 42.4)

103 *Gerard Anne Edwards*, 1732. Oil on canvas, $12\frac{1}{2}$ × $15\frac{5}{8}$ (31.8 × 39.7). The National Trust (Bearsted Collection, Upton House, Warwickshire)

104 *The Edwards Family*, 1733–34. Oil on canvas, 26 × 33 (66 × 83.8). Private Collection. Photo by courtesy of M. Knoedler & Co. Inc., New York

105 *George Arnold*, *c.* 1740. Oil on canvas, $35\frac{5}{8}$ × $27\frac{7}{8}$ (30.5 × 70.8). Reproduced by permission of the Syndics of the Fitzwilliam Museum, Cambridge

106 *Miss Mary Edwards*, 1742. Oil on canvas, $49\frac{3}{8}$ × $39\frac{7}{8}$ (125.4 × 101.3). Copyright the Frick Collection, New York

107 *William James*, *c.* 1740–45. Oil on canvas, $29\frac{1}{2}$ × $24\frac{1}{2}$ (75 × 62.2). Worcester Art Museum, Worcester, Massachusetts

108 *David Garrick as Richard III*, 1745. Oil on canvas, 75 × $98\frac{1}{2}$ (190.5 × 250). The Walker Art Gallery, Liverpool

109 *Frank Matthew Schutz*, *c.* 1755–60. Oil on canvas, $25\frac{1}{4}$ × 30 (64 × 76.2). Private Collection. Photo The Paul Mellon Centre for Studies in British Art

110 *Sir Francis Dashwood at his Devotions*, 1742–46. Oil on canvas, 48 × 35 (122 × 89). Private Collection. Photo The Paul Mellon Centre for Studies in British Art

111 *Lord Grey and Lady Mary West as Children*, 1740. Oil on canvas, $41\frac{1}{2}$ × 35 (105.4 × 89). Washington University Gallery of Art, St Louis, Missouri

112 *Boy in a Green Coat*, *c.* 1756. Oil on canvas, 25 × 19 (63.5 × 48.3). Art Gallery of Ontario, Toronto

113, 114 *The Graham Children*, 1742. Oil on canvas, whole picture $63\frac{3}{4}$ × $71\frac{1}{4}$ (162 × 181). The Tate Gallery, London. Colour photo John Webb

115 JONATHAN RICHARDSON *Francis Godolphin, 2nd Earl of Godolphin.* Oil on canvas, 49 × 39 (124.5 × 99). Yale Center for British Art, Paul Mellon Collection

116 JOSEPH HIGHMORE *Mrs Sharp and Child.* Oil on canvas, 50 × 40 (127 × 101.5). Yale Center for British Art, Paul Mellon Collection

117 ALLAN RAMSAY *Alexander Boswell, Lord Auchinleck*, *c.* 1748–54. Oil on canvas, 50 × 40 (127 × 101.5). Yale Center for British Art, Paul Mellon Collection

118 SIR JOSHUA REYNOLDS *Portrait of an Unknown Man*, 1748. Oil on canvas, 30 × 25 (76 × 63.5). Marble Hill House, Twickenham (Greater London Council)

119 *The Painter and his Pug*, 1745. Oil on canvas, $35\frac{1}{2}$ × $27\frac{1}{2}$ (90 × 70). The Tate Gallery, London. Photo John Webb

120 *The Shrimp Girl*, after 1740. Oil on canvas, 25 × $20\frac{3}{4}$ (63.5 × 52.7). Reproduced by courtesy of the Trustees of the National Gallery, London

121, 122 Plate I of *The Analysis of Beauty*, 1753. Engraving, whole picture $14\frac{5}{8}$ × $19\frac{5}{8}$ (37.1 × 49.8)

123 Plate II of *The Analysis of Beauty*, 1753. Engraving, $14\frac{5}{8}$ × $19\frac{5}{8}$ (37.1 × 49.8)

124–126 *The March to Finchley*, 1746. Oil on canvas, whole picture 40 × $52\frac{1}{2}$ (101.6 × 133.3). The Thomas Coram Foundation for Children, London. Colour photos Eileen Tweedy; black-and-white photo The Paul Mellon Centre for Studies in British Art

127, 128 *The Wedding Dance*, *c.* 1745. Oil on canvas, 27 × $35\frac{1}{2}$ (69.6 × 90.2). London Borough of Southwark, South London Art Gallery; on loan to the Tate Gallery, London. Colour photo Eileen Tweedy

129–131 *Calais Gate, or The Roast Beef of Old England*, 1748. Oil on canvas, 31 × $37\frac{1}{4}$ (78.7 × 94.6). The Tate Gallery, London. Colour photos John Webb

132 Detail of plate 6 of *Industry and Idleness*: see ills. 134–140

133 Detail of *Captain Thomas Coram*: see ill. 101. The Thomas Coram Foundation for Children, London. Photo Eileen Tweedy

134–140 *Industry and Idleness*, 1, 5, 6, 9–12, 1747. Engravings, each $10\frac{1}{4}$ × $13\frac{1}{2}$ (26 × 34.3)

141 *The Four Stages of Cruelty*: 'Cruelty in Perfection', 1751. Woodcut after Hogarth by John Bell, $17\frac{5}{8}$ × $14\frac{7}{8}$ (44.8 × 37.8). Andrew Edmunds

142 *The Four Stages of Cruelty*: 'The Reward of Cruelty', 1751. Engraving, 14 × $11\frac{3}{4}$ (35.6 × 30)

143 *Beer Street*, 1751. Engraving, first state, $14\frac{1}{8}$ × 12 (35.8 × 30.4)

144 *Gin Lane*, 1751. Engraving, $14\frac{1}{8}$ × 12 (35.8 × 30.4)

145 Detail of *The Banquet*, from the *Election* series: see ill.

147. By courtesy of the Trustees of Sir John Soane's Museum, London

146 *The Polling*, from the *Election* series, 1754. Oil on canvas, 40 × 50 (101 × 127). By courtesy of the Trustees of Sir John Soane's Museum, London

147 *The Banquet*, from the *Election* series, 1754. Oil on canvas, 40 × 50 (101 × 127). By courtesy of the Trustees of Sir John Soane's Museum, London

148 Detail of *The Polling*, from the *Election* series: see ill. 146. By courtesy of the Trustees of Sir John Soane's Museum, London

149, 150 *Chairing the Member*, from the *Election* series, 1754. Oil on canvas, whole picture 40 × 50 (101 × 127). By courtesy of the Trustees of Sir John Soane's Museum, London

151 St Mary Redcliffe, Bristol, with Hogarth's altarpiece in its original position: detail of drawing by James Johnson, 1828. Pencil and watercolour, 8 × 5 (20.3 × 12.7). City of Bristol Museum and Art Gallery

152, 153 St Mary Redcliffe Altarpiece, 1755–56. Oil on panel, centre 22′3 × 19′2 (672 × 584), each wing 13′10 × 11′11½ (422 × 364). City of Bristol Museum and Art Gallery, St Nicholas Church Museum

154 *John Pine, c.* 1755. Oil on canvas, 28½ × 24½ (72.4 × 62.2). Collection of the Beaverbrook Art Gallery, Fredericton, New Brunswick

155 *Heads of Six of Hogarth's Servants, c.* 1750–55. Oil on canvas, 24½ × 29½ (62.2 × 75). The Tate Gallery, London

156 *James Caulfield, 1st Earl of Charlemont, c.* 1759. Oil on canvas, 23½ × 19½ (59.7 × 49.5). Smith College Museum of Art, Northampton, Massachusetts (Gift of Mr and Mrs Keith Kane)

157 REMBRANDT *The Artist in his Studio*, late 1620s. Oil on panel, 10 × 12½ (25 × 31.3). Courtesy Museum of Fine Arts, Boston (The Zoe Oliver Sherman Collection)

158 *The Artist painting the Comic Muse*, 1758. Oil on canvas, 15½ × 14¾ (39.4 × 37.5). National Portrait Gallery, London

159 *The Bench*, 1758. Engraving, picture area 6⅝ × 7¾ (16.8 × 19.7)

160 *The Lady's Last Stake*, 1759. Oil on canvas, 36 × 41½ (91.4 × 105.4). Albright-Knox Art Gallery, Buffalo, New York (Seymour H. Knox Fund)

161 *Sigismonda mourning over the Heart of Guiscardo*, 1759. Oil on canvas, 39½ × 49¾ (100.3 × 126.4). The Tate Gallery, London

162 *The Times, Plate I,* 1762. Engraving, 8⅞ × 11⅝ (22.5 × 29.5)

163 *John Wilkes,* 1763. Etching, 12½ × 8¾ (31.7 × 22.2)

164 *The Bruiser, C. Churchill,* 1763. Engraving, 13½ × 10 (34.3 × 25.4)

165 LOUIS FRANÇOIS ROUBILIAC Monument of General Hargrave, 1757. Marble. Westminster Abbey, London. Photo Warburg Institute

166 *The Bathos,* 1764. Engraving, 10¼ × 12⅞ (26 × 32.7)

213

Index

Figures in *italic* are illustration numbers